# A Hundred Years of
# THE MANCHESTER SHIP CANAL

## Ted Gray

A Memories publication

© Ted Gray

This edition published by
Memories,
222 Kings Road,
Firswood,
Manchester M16 OJW,
Tel: 0161 862 9399

Reprint organised by

_Cliff Hayes_

ISBN - 1 899181 85 7

Former ISBN - 1 85926 030 6

Printed and bound by: MFP Design and Print.
Longford Trading Estate,
Thomas Street,
Stretford,
Manchester,
M32 OJT.
Tel: 0161 864 4540.

Cover photograph: *No.9 Dock, Salford, 1972.*

Back cover photograph: *The 'Ocean Transport' seen from Warburton Bridge, 1973.*

Title page photograph: *Barton Aqueduct and the road bridge have been swung to permit the passage of a vessel. A large oil tanker is moored at the Barton Oil Berth.*

# THE AUTHOR

It may be that the Americans are responsible for the author's interest in ships. As a small boy, accompanying his cousin on a Sunday cycle ride in 1941, he found himself on the Flixton side of the Ship Canal near Irlam Locks. An American ship was just pulling out on its way to Manchester, and the sailors, perhaps feeling sorry for the two wartime waifs watching from the bank, threw half-a-dozen oranges ashore. These were rare treasures in the period of food rationing. The oranges were carried home in triumph and offered up with a rather lame explanation of how they had been acquired, for ships did not sail through the district where the boys' parents had instructed them to ride.

The location was revisited on several subsequent occasions in the hope that the experience might be repeated. It wasn't ! But watching the ships passing to or from Liverpool Bay where the North Atlantic convoys assembled, was a moving experience, particularly when a vessel showed scars inflicted by an enemy attack. Though the two boys knew little of the terrible losses caused by U-Boat menace, a great respect and admiration for the bravery of merchant seamen was engendered.

As an evacuee at Lancaster, the author saw ships on a smaller scale on the River Lune and at Glasson Dock, where the small dry dock was kept busy in the war years with repairs to minesweepers. On return home, he joined the Sea Cadets, but never managed to leave dry land. In 1952 the author qualified as a teacher, and (the Ship Canal Company kindly granting a permit for photography) he made a film-strip for use in schools. On the opening of a new school in 1957, the writer was delighted to find that his classroom on the top floor enjoyed a view over the wall by No.7 Dock, where the Prince Line ships berthed. Tours of the docks were arranged regularly as much for the teacher's benefit as for that of the students.

The author's career has included a period as Senior Lecturer in Education at Didsbury College, Manchester, and from 1970 to 1983 he was Headmaster of Walkden High School, Worsley. He holds a degree in Economic History, and has a special interest in local transport matters.

The author and his wife, Kathleen, at Salford Quays, at the side of the former No.8 Dock.

*Ted Gray*

**Previous Publications:–**
'Tramways of Salford,' 'Trafford Park Tramways,' 'Salford City Transport,' 'The Manchester Carriage & Tramways Company,' 'Greetings From Salford,' 'Greetings From Eccles,' and contributions to a civic history and a number of transport journals.

Before the Ship Canal was constructed, small boats came to Manchester via the rivers. A painting by Day Jackson, dated 1856, looks downstream from Albert Bridge, New Bailey Street, the Manchester Bank on the left, with warehouses and river flats moored alongside. The bridge in the distance is that of the 1830 Liverpool and Manchester Railway. The intermediate crossings at Irwell Street and Prince's Bridge were not built until 1877 and 1863 respectively.

*(Reproduced by courtesy of the City of Salford Museums & Art Gallery)*

Grain Wharf, Mariners canal, and the Victoria office complex in the Salford Quays development on the site of the former terminal docks.

# ACKNOWLEDGEMENTS

The writer warmly acknowledges the co-operation of the Manchester Ship Canal Company, particularly for permission to reproduce photographs from the Company's archives and to quote from the house journal *'Port Of Manchester Review'*. Also, the kind interest of the Chairman, Robert Hough, in contributing the Foreword is much appreciated.

Anyone attempting to write about the construction period of the canal must rely heavily upon the two-volume history by a former auditor to the Company and ex-Lord Mayor of Manchester, Sir Bosdin Leech. Published in 1907, Leech's *'History Of The Manchester Ship Canal'* is a definitive record of the struggles and achievements of the Victorian period. For twentieth century history, the several publications of the Company itself provided details of the working practices of the port. Contributors to the annual editions of the *'Port Of Manchester Review'* covered many diverse topics, some of which (such as dredging, ship control, work of the tugboatmen, pilots, dock police, etc.) might otherwise have remained unrecorded. These, and other publications consulted, are listed in the bibliography.

The illustrations come mainly from the author's collection, assembled over some 40 years from a variety of sources, but principally from the Company's Public Relations Department, whose staff have tolerated an interested amateur's assorted queries and requests since 1950. From D.A.St.John Hollis and Brian Vaughton to David Thornley and David Hastie, all have been most courteous and helpful, and their many kindnesses have been greatly appreciated. Photographers for the Company have included Stewart Bale of Liverpool, R.L.Offley of Ellesmere Port, Airviews, Elsam Mann & Cooper, Entwistle Thorpe, Fotaire, and Mack's, all of Manchester. Commercial postcard photographers provided a valuable source of historical material, and examples have been included from J.L.Brown, Charles Downs, A.H.Clarke, Harry Grundy, J.F.Lawrence, Lilywhite Ltd., R.M.Morris, T.Pinder, and Raymond Sankey of Barrow. As the photographs were acquired over a period of time, it is regretted that the source was not always noted, and apologies are offered in case of any inadvertent omission in these credits. Some photographs in the period since 1950 were taken by the writer himself, courtesy of a permit from the Ship Canal Company. D.Rendell Photographic Services of Hale prepared many prints. Some of the colour pictures are from original transparencies by Brian Vaughton. Alan Palmer of Worsley drew the maps and the illustration of a Mersey & Irwell sailing flat.

Acknowledgement is made to R.Alexander of the Furness Withy Group, for information on the Prince Line; R.B.Stoker and Norman Edwards Associates (Manchester Liners); Greater Manchester County Record Office; staff of H.M.Customs & Excise, Manchester, and the Maritime Museum, Liverpool, for access to the shipping registers; Trafford Library; Douglas Britton, former member of the Dock Police, who kindly made available his copies of the *'Review'*; Bill Turner, ex-Dock Office staff; George Norman; Bill Fereday; Lengthline Ltd.; R. Mewha; T.J.B.Whiteley; and Andrew Cross, who drew attention to the 1885 poem *'The Manchester Ship Canal'* quoted in The Oxford Book Of English Traditional Verse. As always, the writer is grateful to the staff of the Salford Local History Library.

The first section of the book tells the story of the early waterways to Manchester, after which the history of the construction and operation of the Ship Canal is related in the captions to the illustrations, which are arranged, as far as possible, in chronological order.

Although the compilation has been a labour of love, the initial idea, encouragement, and subsequent guidance came from Cliff Hayes, who also sought out some additional source material. Once again, the writer is indebted to his wife Kathleen, for support, encouragement and tolerance of household disruption during the lengthy process of sorting, sifting, and assembling material into some sort of order. To his son Robert, he offers heartfelt thanks for introducing him to the invaluable word processor.

*Ted Gray, Salford 1993.*

# FOREWORD

With 1994 marking the centenary of the opening of the Manchester Ship Canal, *A Hundred Years of the Manchester Ship Canal* is a most timely publication and I wish it well. The saga of how those Victorian pioneers strove to overcome daunting difficulties to realise their vision of a seaway to Manchester and succeeded so magnificently is indeed stirring.

Furthermore, the photographs with which the author illustrates these themes are themselves an important record and contribute significantly to our understanding.

The compelling story of how the Manchester Ship Canal has weathered change, evolved and adapted and is now confidently moving forward into the next hundred years is well worth telling.

*Robert Hough*

Robert Hough
Chairman, Manchester Ship Canal Company

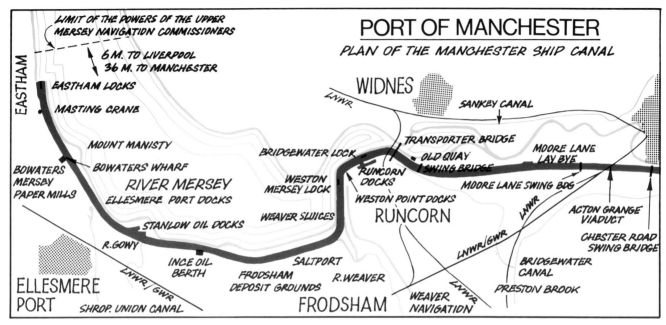

# PORT OF MANCHESTER
## PLAN OF THE MANCHESTER SHIP CANAL

LIMIT OF THE POWERS OF THE UPPER
MERSEY NAVIGATION COMMISSIONERS

6 M. TO LIVERPOOL
36 M. TO MANCHESTER

EASTHAM

EASTHAM LOCKS

MASTING CRANE

MOUNT MANISTY

BOWATERS WHARF

BOWATERS
MERSEY
PAPER MILLS

RIVER MERSEY
ELLESMERE PORT DOCKS

STANLOW OIL DOCKS

R. GOWY

INCE OIL
BERTH

ELLESMERE
PORT

LNWR / GWR

SHROP. UNION CANAL

FRODSHAM
DEPOSIT GROUNDS

SALTPORT

R. WEAVER

FRODSHAM

WEAVER SLUICES

WESTON
MERSEY LOCK

BRIDGEWATER LOCK

WESTON POINT DOCKS

RUNCORN
DOCKS

RUNCORN

WEAVER
NAVIGATION

LNWR

LNWR / GWR

WIDNES

LNWR

SANKEY CANAL

TRANSPORTER BRIDGE

OLD QUAY
SWING BRIDGE

MOORE LANE
LAY BYE

MOORE LANE SWING BDG.

ACTON GRANGE
VIADUCT

CHESTER ROAD
SWING BRIDGE

BRIDGEWATER
CANAL

PRESTON BROOK

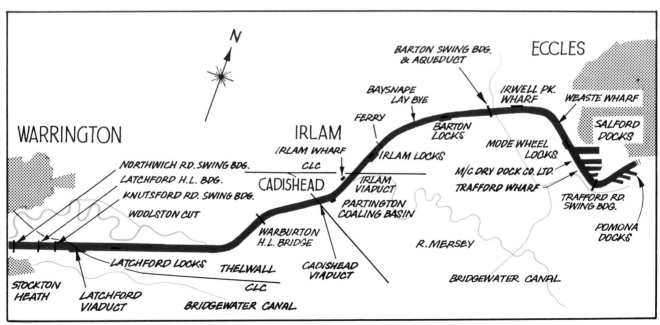

N

WARRINGTON

NORTHWICH RD. SWING BDG.
LATCHFORD H.L. BDG.
KNUTSFORD RD. SWING BDG.
WOOLSTON CUT

STOCKTON
HEATH

LATCHFORD
VIADUCT

LATCHFORD LOCKS

THELWALL

CLC

BRIDGEWATER CANAL

WARBURTON
H.L. BRIDGE

CADISHEAD
VIADUCT

CADISHEAD

IRLAM WHARF
CLC

IRLAM

FERRY

IRLAM LOCKS

IRLAM
VIADUCT

PARTINGTON
COALING BASIN

BAYSNAPE
LAY BYE

BARTON SWING BDG.
& AQUEDUCT

BARTON
LOCKS

IRWELL PK.
WHARF

ECCLES

WEASTE WHARF

SALFORD
DOCKS

MODE WHEEL
LOCKS

M/C DRY DOCK CO. LTD.

TRAFFORD WHARF

TRAFFORD RD.
SWING BDG.

POMONA
DOCKS

R. MERSEY

BRIDGEWATER CANAL

Many ships passed along the canal during the hours of darkness. The motor vessel 'HALIA' is seen at Eastham Locks in 1981.

The vessel 'MAJ RAGNE' passes the cranes of the container terminal as she prepares to berth in No.9 Dock in 1973.

The engine room telegraphs of the steam tug 'DANIEL ADAMSON'. The vessel was built in 1903 for the Shropshire Union Canal, and was then named 'RALPH BROCKLEBANK'. It is now preserved at the Ellesmere Port Boat Museum.

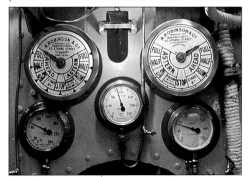

# INTRODUCTION

ONE HUNDRED YEARS AGO, the construction of the Manchester ship Canal was hailed as one of the greatest engineering achievements of the Victorian era. In earlier years, small vessels had been able to reach Manchester by way of the rivers Mersey and Irwell, and in 1776 the Bridgewater Canal offered another route to the tidal estuary at Runcorn. Nevertheless, because of the high cost of transhipping goods through the port of Liverpool, the nineteenth century saw a growing demand for a better waterway to enable large sea-going ships to reach the heart of Industrial Lancashire.

Several schemes were proposed and considered, some of which involved improving and enlarging the existing river navigation, whilst others favoured a barrage across the Mersey, or a tidal canal all the way to Manchester. The success of the Suez Canal project, which was completed in 1869, inspired those advocating a deep and wide waterway to Manchester, and efforts were redoubled to find an acceptable scheme which would be approved by Parliament.

After several earlier plans had come to nought, there took place in 1882 the famous meeting called by Daniel Adamson at his home in Didsbury. This resulted in the formation of the Provisional Committee, which commissioned a detailed survey of the route of a possible waterway. Bosdin Leech, a supporter of the scheme and auditor to the Company (later to be Lord Mayor of Manchester, knighted soon after the canal was opened, and writer of the definitive history of the early years), personally visited all existing ship canals in Holland, Belgium, the Baltic, Canada and Suez to compile information. The promoters had to fight the determined opposition of Liverpool and the railway companies, overcome scepticism, raise funds, and gain Parliamentary approval, which they did at the third attempt in 1885. Work began in 1887. Considerable difficulties and set-backs were encountered along the way, but the full length of the Manchester Ship Canal was open for sea-going vessels from the 1st of January, 1894.

The Canal's important role in facilitating the prosperity of manufacturing industries in the North-West of England may be assessed by the fact that in the early years of the twentieth century, average freight charges on imported goods had dropped to about one-third of what they had been twenty-five years earlier. Tonnage handled rose steadily, reaching a peak in the 1950s, since when containerisation, contraction of manufacturing industry, and changes in cargoes, size of ships, and patterns of trade have all played a part in the decline of traffic. Whilst the Canal from Runcorn to the Mersey estuary has continued nonetheless to handle considerable tonnages and to contribute significantly both to the economy of the region and to the prosperity of the Company, in the early 1980s there seemed little prospect of a revival of business on the upper reaches and the terminal docks at Salford fell largely into disuse. The past decade, however, has seen the implementation of the impressive and prestigious Salford Quays development project, regenerating the derelict docklands, and fittingly demonstrating that same vitality and imagination that so characterised those Victorian pioneers a hundred years ago.

# CONTENTS

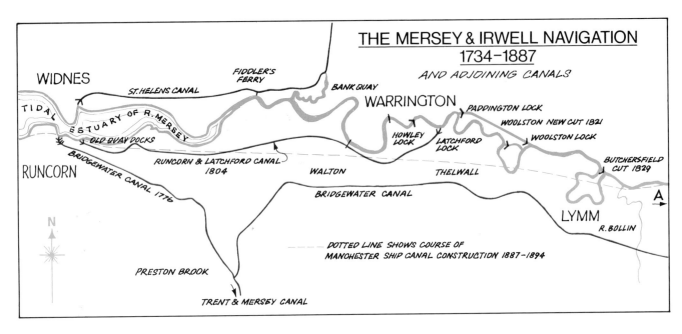

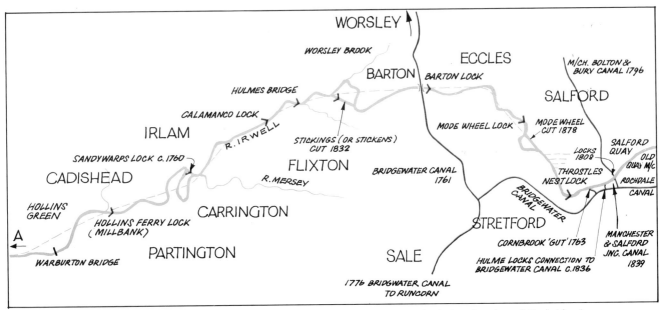

Map of the Mersey & Irwell Navigation system 1734–1887. (Drawn by Alan Palmer, based on Leech and Corbridge.)

# EARLY WATERWAYS TO MANCHESTER

The 'Industrial Revolution' is generally considered to have begun about 1760, but long before this date Manchester had become the centre of a web of industrial settlements, mainly located in the foothills of the Pennines. The commercial success of these growing enterprises depended upon efficient transport arrangements for the carriage of raw materials and the distribution of finished products. Packhorses and horse-drawn carts soon proved inadequate to meet demands, and unsurfaced roads, which were frequently impassable in wet weather, led to the increased use of river navigations. The route along the courses of the Mersey and Irwell, however, had considerable disadvantages. Both rivers were frequently short of water, silted up regularly, and had many mudbanks and assorted obstacles along their lengths, all of which led to delay and unreliability in the transport of goods. As early as 1660 suggestions had been made that the rivers Mersey and Irwell should be cleared and dredged to make them more easily navigable. The estuary of the Mersey had been used by ships from early times, but Warrington was the effective limit of navigation. Thomas Patten, a merchant who had removed obstructions in the tideway to allow his barges to reach Bank Quay, Warrington, had also drawn attention to the advantages to be gained by making the rivers navigable as far as Manchester. Nothing had been done immediately, but the idea was revived in 1710, and in 1712 Thomas Steers published his scheme ("surveyed by order of the Gentlemen at Manchester") for straightening, dredging and deepening the rivers to allow ships to sail from Bank Quay, Warrington, to Hunts Bank, Manchester. Vessels were able to sail as far as Warrington on the tidal portion of the Mersey Estuary, and from that point Steers' plan involved the construction of a tow-path (for men or horses to haul the boats when they could not use sail), and eight sets of locks and weirs, the latter to ensure a constant depth of water in each section, and the locks to lift the ships to Manchester's height above sea-level. It was claimed that the scheme would be "beneficial to trade, advantageous to the poor, and convenient for the carriage of coals, stone, timber, wares and merchandises."

Several Manchester businessmen were ready to support the project, but the Act enabling work to commence was not obtained until 1721. Even then, the plan did not materialise for some time, probably because the financial failures of the 'South Sea Bubble' period were still fresh in the minds of potential investors. The project eventually began to take shape in 1724, but progress was slow because of the shallow and winding nature of stretches of the rivers. Thus it was that the Mersey and Irwell Navigation Company made the first attempt to provide Manchester with a reliable outlet to the sea. By 1734 ships of up to 50 tons were able

The River Navigation Company's lock at Mode Wheel (named 'Maud Wheel' on early plans) was constructed close to an existing weir, which provided a head of water to power the wheel in the flour and logwood mill on the Salford bank on the left. The photograph was taken in 1888, looking upstream towards the future site of the Ship Canal's terminal docks. It shows the detail of the lock gates and the timbers protecting the stonework. The lamp on the central pier was to assist navigation after dark. The well-worn tow-path separates the mill wall from the lockside.

to sail to the city. Steers' plan had been followed fairly closely. The highest lock on the Irwell was built at Throstle Nest, a little way upstream from Trafford Road. Others, such as those at Mode Wheel and Barton, were built alongside existing weirs, at points where water-mills had been established for a considerable time. At these points, the mill-owners occasionally made life difficult for the bargemen by running-out too much water and thereby reducing the depth of water in the upper reaches. The lock which admitted boats to and from the tidal section of the Mersey was at Howley, east of Bank Quay, Warrington, a distance of some 22 miles from Manchester.

The vessels used on the Mersey & Irwell Navigation were known as 'flats.' They were small sailing craft, capable of working in the estuary and along the coast. The early 'flats' drew only five feet of water, and were built with a beam of about 12 feet to fit the 15½ feet-wide locks. Later, some of the locks were enlarged to admit boats of greater beam and draught, though the dimensions of vessels coming all the way to Manchester were governed by the 70½ feet long Calamanco Lock, near Irlam. This lock, although improvements were planned, was never extended, and consequently through loads were limited to about 50 tons. Masts could be lowered to enable 'flats' to pass under the bridges at Barton and Warrington, and, although assisted by sails, the winding nature of the course meant that the boats were usually pulled by men or horses for much of the distance. The tow-path changed sides at several points, and arrangements had to be made for the hauliers to cross by bridge or ferry. Users of the new waterway paid a toll of 3s 4d (16½p) per ton, a charge which remained unaltered for a century and a half.

Merchants were slow to take advantage of the new navigation, and traffic was sparse in the first few years because of the still-uncertain state of the two rivers. For a time, there were only five boats in regular use. The Company sought ways to make the navigation more attractive and reliable, and dug 'cuts' to shorten the route by avoiding long meanders. Improved facilities were provided by 1740 on a wharf near Water Street, at the end of Quay Street, Manchester. A second Quay Street, on the opposite bank of the river, off Chapel Street, is a reminder of the location of the Salford Quay Company's wharves, which lay between New Bailey Bridge and Blackfriars Bridge. The number of quays and warehouses along the Irwell increased, but the Company paid no dividends in the early years, and not until 1753 did the undertaking appear to be on a sound financial basis.

The vessels used on the Mersey & Irwell river navigation were small sailing barges known as 'flats.' Their dimensions were such as to fit the locks, and their strong timbers enabled them to withstand frequent groundings on the mudbanks. The mast, hinged at deck-level so as to be lowered when passing under bridges, supported a sail, but because of the winding nature of the rivers, it was more usual for the boats to be hauled by men or horses. The 'flats' were crewed usually by two men and a boy. (Drawing by Alan Palmer.)

In 1758 came the first plan of the Duke of Bridgewater for a canal from Worsley to Manchester. Work commenced at Worsley in the following year, and the Duke purchased 14 acres of land on the Salford bank of the Irwell, an area intended as a terminus from which barges could join the river navigation by means of two locks. The Mersey & Irwell Navigation Company, previously opposed to a canal scheme which would have drawn water from the Irwell and diminished their supply, raised no objection. An Act of 1737 had given the Company permission to make Worsley Brook navigable for two miles from the Irwell to the Duke's coal-mining area, but, lacking funds at that time, nothing had been done. The Duke's own project did not need to steal water from the Company's supply, and being constructed without locks, his canal would be cheaper than the Worsley Brook scheme. The Company saw benefits in increased traffic from the Duke's plan to link his canal with the river navigation, and agreed a preferential rate of 6d per ton, with the proviso that other boat-owners, paying the higher rates, should take precedence over the Duke's barges when passing through locks.

Work on the Bridgewater Canal had begun at Worsley Mill by March 1759. James Brindley joined the Duke's team of advisers in the summer of that year, about which time there was a dramatic change of plan. The Duke considered the possibility of capturing the Cheshire and, eventually, the Liverpool carrying trade. Consequently, it was decided to change the route of the canal to carry it over the river navigation at Barton, so as to approach Manchester from the Stretford side, and to include a short branch at Longford Bridge to connect with the main road to Chester. The crossing of the river, flowing at a much lower level, could have been achieved by building a flight of locks on each side. This would have been the conventional method, but it was costly in both construction and maintenance, and time-consuming for boatmen in terms of the delay occasioned by the operation of locking through. Instead of locks, Brindley proposed the bold plan of taking the canal over the river by means of an aqueduct, though the

idea of one vessel sailing over the top of another was regarded as unrealistic by some critics. However, the Duke was prepared to try Brindley's scheme. By mid-1760 the first length of the canal was in use as far as Barton, at which point it was sealed whilst the aqueduct was constructed. The Duke used the Company's river navigation to bring timber, stone, bricks and other building materials to the site, and a crane was installed on the parapet so that coal brought along the canal from the Worsley mines could be lowered in twig baskets to the river barges below, and thence conveyed to Manchester.

Brindley's stone aqueduct was crossed by a vessel for the first time on the 17th July 1761. The Bridgewater Canal

Brindley's stone aqueduct at Barton, which carried the Bridgewater Canal across the river navigation, was used for the first time on the 17th July 1761. As the canal was not completed as far as Manchester until 1764, coal from the Worsley mines was transferred at this point from canal barges to river 'flats' by means of a crane on the parapet. The engraving is from Aitken's 'History Of Manchester' 1795, and shows the view upstream, where a weir (to power the wheel in Bardsley's Mill on the Trafford Park bank, right) may be seen through the arches of the aqueduct. Barton locks were beyond the arch on the left, where the tow-path of the old waterway passes beneath the aqueduct on a wooden platform. The peculiar timber construction under the right-hand arch was a social room provided for the navigators ('navvies') engaged on building the canal. It was offered in compensation for the shortage of hostelries in the neighbourhood. The room became disused after the departure of the 'navvies,' and was eventually dismantled.

demonstrated that canals need not depend upon the courses of other natural waterways. Indeed, the boats struggling through the shallows on the river navigation below seemed to emphasise the superiority of the canal. The Duke's arrangement for a link with the river navigation survived, but the site was changed to Cornbrook where a connection (known as 'The Gut') was made with the Irwell in 1763, as work on the canal approached Manchester. Difficulties regarding land ownership were resolved by the Duke purchasing the Hulme Hall Estates, and the Castlefield terminus of the Bridgewater Canal was reached in the following year, though it was 1765 before its wharves were ready to sell Worsley coal. In the meantime, most of the coal had been carried to the city by using the crane at Barton to transfer loads from the canal barges to the river navigation 'flats', a practice which continued on the Salford side until the end of the century. The Duke, in fact, held shares in both the Mersey & Irwell Navigation Company and the Salford Quay Company, an independent concern, and he continued to run 'flats' on the rivers after the opening of his own canal.

Even before the Bridgewater Canal reached Manchester, the Duke's intention of continuing the 'cut' from Stretford to the Mersey Estuary had become clear. The Mersey & Irwell Navigation Company then recognised the danger from the Duke's competition, and opposed the scheme. The Duke argued that the old river navigation was expensive and unreliable, and that boats were not able to reach the entrance lock at Warrington except at very high tides. He gained the support of the merchants by forecasting a reduction in tolls. Evidence emerged that there were some 20 sailing 'flats' regularly using the river navigation as far as the Manchester and Salford quays, but that a voyage from Liverpool could, on occasions, take over a week, and that the vessels had to reduce their tonnage in summer because of shortage of water. The House of Commons, whilst ready to sanction a new competing canal, was not prepared to consider any scheme which would take water from streams feeding the river navigation, so the Duke was obliged to prove that he could obtain an adequate supply from the soughs draining his coal mines. Thus it was that the Bridgewater Canal was extended to Preston Brook by 1771, and to Runcorn by 1776, some 17 years after the commencement at Worsley. The journey from Manchester was about 30 miles long. The Duke's canal avoided locks by following the contours of the land or by building embankments, but from the terminal wharves at Runcorn a steep flight of ten locks was necessary to enable barges to enter the Mersey Estuary, from where they could be towed across open water to Liverpool. The Duke thus broke the Mersey & Irwell Navigation Company's monopoly of water carriage to Manchester, and provided a route free of tides, floods, shallows and, except at Runcorn, locks. Barges without sails replaced many of the sailing 'flats' and Runcorn became an important point for transhipment. The Mersey & Irwell Navigation Company, despairing of their slower and unreliable

Barton Locks on the old river navigation were sited on the Eccles bank, immediately upstream from the point where Brindley's aqueduct carried the Bridgewater Canal over the Irwell. In this view, looking downstream, part of the original road bridge may be glimpsed through the arch of the aqueduct. In the building to the right were the stables. The towing horses were changed at this, and several other points along the waterway. The river locks were destroyed in 1891 during the construction of the Ship Canal, and the new Barton Locks were established further downstream.

route, offered to sell their undertaking to the Duke for £10,000. The offer was rejected, for the Duke preferred to join forces with the independent Salford Quay company, of which he became sole owner in 1779.

When the Bridgewater connection to the Mersey was complete, the earlier concern was dubbed the 'Old Navigation,' or the 'Old Quay Company.' It passed into the control of a group of Manchester and Liverpool businessmen, who were determined to make the river system succeed. Trade was increasing, and it was thought that there was sufficient traffic for both the Duke's canal and the river navigation to share. The new owners engaged engineers to report on possible improvements, and subsequently faults were remedied, new 'cuts' were made to shorten the route, and locks were rebuilt and enlarged. One writer recorded that "the winding course of the river has been corrected by cuts across the necks of principal bends." Another major problem lay outside the navigation and was caused by the shifting channels of the Mersey estuary, where low tides or adverse winds often prevented the 'flats' from reaching the entrance lock at Warrington. The solution to this particular difficulty was found in the construction of a new canal, about 8 miles long, cut from Latchford (above the old entrance lock) seawards to Runcorn, where a new lock allowed vessels to join or leave the Mersey at a point where there was a good depth of water at high tides. This location gained the title of 'Old Quay.' (The Company's yards and warehouses on Water Street, Manchester, were also known as the 'Old Quay.' The 'New Quay Company,' private carriers, who included boat-

An advertisement for the Duke Of Bridgewater's Canal indicates the range of operations and its connections via other canals to distant parts of the country. The list of independent carriers includes Thomas Pickford.

Tidmarsh's drawing of the Irwell Quays from Albert Bridge, New Bailey Street, Manchester

building amongst their activities, also had premises on Water Street, close to Regent Bridge. It was the New Quay Company's boatyard which was later the scene of a disaster in 1828, when a new 'flat,' the 'Emma,' planned to have been the largest vessel on the river, overturned on launching, drowning some 33 persons who had been on deck.)

With the opening of the Runcorn and Latchford Canal in 1804 (the 'Old Quay Canal') a period of prosperity seemed assured. Rivalry with the Bridgewater Canal resulted in various inducements to traders to use one or the other system, but traffic continued to increase and identical tolls were agreed in a bid to end ruinous competition. The monopoly thus created by the two companies began to be challenged after 1812, when the number of independent carriers increased, their competition leading to a reduction in freight charges. Even so, trade prospered on both waterways.

The Mersey & Irwell Navigation Company advertised the cutting of their new Runcorn and Latchford Canal ("at a great expence") in a Manchester Directory of 1804.

It was usual for 'flats' from Liverpool to sail with the incoming tide, the current pushing them along to Runcorn. On reaching Runcorn, some would enter the 'Old Quay' canal through the new lock, and then take 14 or 15 hours to reach Manchester via the river navigation, changing tow-horses four times on the way. Others would move through the Bridgewater locks to join the rival system. Tonnage increased so much that occasionally there was an insufficient number of vessels available to carry all cargoes. It was recorded that sometimes as many as 40 or 50 'flats' left Liverpool on one tide. The new lock at Runcorn was often unable to admit all these vessels during the period of high water, so enlarged facilities were constructed with two locks and two dock basins, which, by 1825, were capable of dealing with 140 vessels at each tide. It was estimated that there were some 250 'flats' at work on the Bridgewater Canal and the river navigation combined, of which total the Company owned about 70. With the new facilities, larger coastal vessels were able to dock at Runcorn, where their cargoes were often transhipped to 'flats' to go further upriver. More warehouses and further improvements were incorporated along the navigation. In 1821 a new canal was cut at Woolston to shorten and widen a difficult section of the old course, and further 'cuts' were made at Butchersfield (Rixton) in 1829 and Stickens (Davyhulme) in 1832. Over the years, these improvements reduced the sailing distance from Albert Bridge, Manchester, to Old Quay, Runcorn, from about 38 miles by the old river course to 27 miles by the navigable channels.

The first record of steamships being used for passengers between Liverpool and Runcorn is in 1815–16, but these early steamers were not capable of towing laden barges across the tideway. Some years later, with the development of more reliable steam-powered boats, the Company began to use steam tugs to tow barges across the estuary, or to assist 'flats' in unfavourable winds. It is thought that the Company first hired steamers, such as the paddle tug 'Eagle' of 1824, and later placed orders for their own steam-powered vessels. The Company's first steam tug was the 'Hercules' in 1830, with engines provided by Bateman & Sherratt of Salford, and in the following year the barge 'Mallory' was converted, but proved unsuccessful, However, three more steam tugs ('Pilot,' 'Rival,' and 'Tower') were in service by 1836. Their use in the estuary made it possible to dismantle much of the sailing gear on the old 'flats,' thereby increasing their carrying capacity. New 'flats' were built to improved designs. The Bridgewater undertaking followed suit in 1839, when their first steam tug, the 'Alice,' was launched.

The use of steam tugs for towing barges on the river and canal navigations was rejected, however. On the river, a greater depth of water was deemed necessary, and, in any event, the numerous bends and locks would have been difficult to negotiate for a vessel

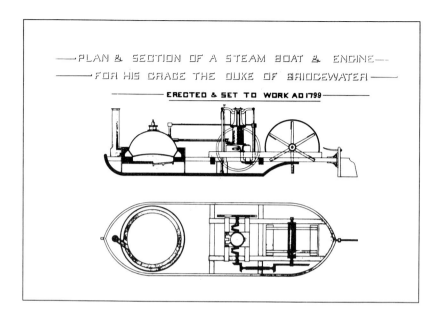

PLAN & SECTION OF A STEAM BOAT & ENGINE — FOR HIS GRACE THE DUKE OF BRIDGEWATER —

ERECTED & SET TO WORK AD 1799

### PASSAGE BOATS.

Two elegant Passage-boats, *Peter Collins* and *Thomas Wilbington*, masters, for passengers and their luggage only, go alternately from Manchester to Runcorn, in Cheshire, one of which leaves Castle-quay, Manchester, every morning at eight o'clock ; passes Altrincham at ten o'clock, London-bridge, near Warrington, at one o'clock (where coaches meet it to convey passengers to Warrington and Liverpool); passes Preston Brook, near Frodsham, at three o'clock (where a stage coach meets it to convey passengers to Chester), and arrives at Runcorn at five o'clock in the evening.

One leaves Runcorn every morning at ten o'clock ; passes Preston Brook at eleven o'clock (where it takes passengers from the Chester coach) ; passes London-bridge at nine o'clock (where it takes up passengers from the Liverpool and Warrington coaches); passes Altrincham at four o'clock. and arrives at Castle-quay, Manchester, at six o'clock in the evening.

Another Passage-boat, *John Renshaw*, master, sets off from London-bridge, near Warrington, every Saturday morning at five o'clock, and brings passengers to Manchester market ; passes Lymn at six o'clock, Altrincham at eight o'clock, and arrives at Manchester at ten o'clock in the morning, and observes the same evening at four o'clock, arrives at Altrincham at six o'clock, Lymn at eight o'clock, and at London-bridge at nine o'clock.

Another Passage-boat, *Nicholas Timperley*, master, from the 29th of September to the 25th of March, leaves Worsley at half past seven o'clock in the morning, and arrives at Manchester at ten o'clock ; returns at half past four o'clock, and arrives at Worsley at seven o'clock the same evening ; and from the 25th of March to the 29th of September, leaves Worsley at seven o'clock in the morning, and arrives at Manchester at nine o'clock ; returns at ten o'clock, and arrives at Worsley at half past twelve o'clock. Also, at three o'clock (except Sunday, and on that day at four o'clock), and arrives at Manchester at five o'clock ; returns to Worsley at half past eight o'clock, where it arrives at eight o'clock. The above boat goes to Leigh every Monday

#### FARES.

| FRONT ROOM. | s. | d. | BACK ROOM. | s. | d. |
|---|---|---|---|---|---|
| To Stretford | 1 | 0 | | 0 | 6 |
| To Altrincham | 1 | 0 | | 0 | 9 |
| To Dunham | 1 | 6 | | 1 | 0 |
| To Lymn | 2 | 0 | | 1 | 3 |
| To London-bridge | 2 | 6 | | 1 | 6 |
| To Preston | 3 | 0 | | 2 | 3 |
| To Runcorn | 3 | 6 | | 2 | 3 |
| To Worsley | 1 | 0 | | 0 | 6 |
| To and from Worsley | 1 | 6 | | 0 | 9 |

with a string of barges in tow. On the Bridgewater Canal, the Duke himself had commissioned a steamboat as early as 1796, the mechanical portions being manufactured by Bateman & Sherratt and fitted into a hull built by Benjamin Powell at Worsley. On trial, the steamboat had hauled eight barges from Worsley to Manchester, but had proved slower than the horse-drawn boats, taking some eight hours on the journey. It was feared that the turbulence caused by the stern paddle wheel would damage the banks and lining of the canal. The Duke's boatmen had derisively named the steamboat 'Buonaparte,' in reference to Napoleon's ambitions, and remained fiercely loyal to their horses. To their delight, the experiment had been abandoned, though Sherratt's engine, re-christened 'Old Nancy,' was removed for use as a pumping engine elsewhere, and the hull was later broken up at Worsley. The Duke, however, was impressed by seeing a model of the 'Charlotte Dundas,' the first successful canal steamer in 1801, and he ordered eight similar steamboats. Sadly, he died in 1803 before they had been built, and his officials cancelled the order, fearing that they would be unpopular with the boatmen.

Passengers had been carried on the Bridgewater Canal between Worsley and Manchester, and between Manchester and Lymm, since 1766. The service was later extended to Runcorn, and a directory of 1788 notes that the Duke has "two elegant passage boats for passengers and their luggage only," one leaving Castlefield (Manchester) at 8.00 a.m., connecting with the Liverpool stage-coach at Warrington by 1.00 p.m., the Chester coach at Preston Brook by 3.00 p.m., and arriving at Runcorn to meet the Liverpool boat at 5.00 p.m. In the other direction, the boat from Runcorn left between 9.00 and 10.00 a.m., picking up passengers from the stage-coaches en route, and arriving in Manchester about 6.00 p.m. The cost was calculated at one penny per mile. The boats offered a smoother and safer ride than the stage coaches, and refreshments could be enjoyed en route without time-wasting stoppages. Times of departure varied slightly over the years, as the journey time was reduced.

This notice for the packet-boats on the Bridgewater Canal appeared in 1804. The 'London Bridge' listed in the fare table is that at Warrington.

Not until May 1807 did the Mersey & Irwell Company offer competing passenger services along the river navigation. The horse-drawn packet-boats left Manchester from the wharf by New Bailey Street bridge (site of the present 'Mark Addy' public house), said to be the busiest spot on the river. The daily departure was at 8.00 a.m., reaching Runcorn at 4.00 p.m. In the other direction, a boat left Runcorn at 10.00 a.m. in summer, 8.00 a.m. in winter, arriving in Manchester eight hours later. To travel between Manchester and Runcorn cost 2s3d (11½p) in the after-cabin or 3s6d (18p) in the fore-cabin. As with the Bridgewater services, the boats connected with the stage-coaches and estuary ferries, and would stop at any of the riverside wharves along the route if required. Steamships for passengers were introduced on the 20-mile estuary section between Liverpool and Runcorn in 1816. New, faster boats, drawn by two horses ridden by "jockey-boys," were later introduced on the river navigation route, being timed to leave Manchester so as to arrive in Runcorn at high-water and connect without delay with the Liverpool steamer. Sir George Head compared the journeys offered by the rival companies in 1835. He recorded that the Bridgewater packet boat at Runcorn was always moored at the summit of the flight of locks, so it was necessary for passengers from Liverpool to toil with their luggage up the slope to the level

**WORSLEY, Nov. 11, 1837.**

Sir,

I have to request that Directions may be given, to enforce Mr. Bradshaw's REGULATION against Flatmen's and Lightermen's WIVES living and sleeping on board with their Husbands.

In explanation of this Order, I want it to be stated, that the existence of such a practice, besides affording many excuses for depredation, leads to a system of Morals extremely detrimental and therefore to be avoided.

I am, your obedient Servant,

JAMES LOCH.

G. S. FEREDAY SMITH, Esq.
*Bridgewater Canal Office,*
*Manchester.*

## MERSEY AND IRWELL NAVIGATION.

*Office at the Old Quay, Water-street.*—*Thomas Lingard, Agent.*

Goods are conveyed by the Company of Proprietors of this navigation daily (Sundays excepted) to and from Manchester and Liverpool and the intermediate places, with the greatest dispatch and safety, and forwarded, by canal or land carriage, to Ashton, Oldham, Stockport, Rochdale, Leeds, Huddersfield, Halifax, Wakefield, Sheffield, and all parts of Yorkshire.

Sloops or vessels, having cargoes to forward by this navigation, are admitted free of dockage into the canal at Runcorn, to discharge their cargoes into the Company's vessels plying on their navigation, as also into their newly-erected Wet Dock, Old Quay, Liverpool.

Elegant and commodious packet-boats, for passengers and their luggage, sail every morning to and from Manchester and Runcorn. The Liverpool Coaches meet the packet at Warrington; and there is a new and commodious steam packet at Runcorn, which meets the company's packets for the conveyance of passengers, &c. to and from Liverpool. Private rooms, for the accommodation of parties, may be engaged for the day.

The following tables shew the time of the sailing and arrival of the packets at Manchester, Warrington and Runcorn, both in summer and winter.

| DOWNWARDS. | SUM. | WIN. | UPWARDS. | SUM. | WIN. |
|---|---|---|---|---|---|
| | h. m. | h. m. | | h. m. | h. m. |
| Boat sails from Manchester | 8  0M. | 8  0M. | Boat sails from Runcorn | 10  0M. | 8  0 |
| Arrives at Warrington | 1  55A. | 1  45A. | Arrives at Warrington | 11  45 | 9  45 |
| Leaves Warrington | 2  0 | 2  0 | Leaves Warrington | 12  0 | 10  0 |
| Arrives at Runcorn | 4  0 | 4  0 | Arrives at Manchester | 6  0 | 4  0 |

| FARES. | Fore Cabin. | After Cabin. |
|---|---|---|
| | s. d. | s. d. |
| From Manchester to Warrington | 2  6 | 1  6 |
| From Manchester to Runcorn | 3  6 | 2  3 |
| From Runcorn to Warrington | 1  0 | 0  9 |

The Committee meet at the Old Quay-office, Manchester, the first Wednesday in the month, and at the Old Quay-office, Liverpool, the second Wednesday in the month, for the dispatch of business.

Shipper at Manchester .......John Barber
Agent at Liverpool ... ...William Guyton
Agent at Warrington...............James Dawson
Agent at Runcorn ...................Samuel Wylde

This Company are also carriers upon the Manchester, Bolton, and Bury canal, and convey goods to all parts on the line, and forward, by other carriers, to places beyond its limits; viz. Chorley, Blackburn, Haslingden, &c.—Joseph Addison, agent, Canal Warehouse, Oldfield-road, Salford, and bottom of King-street.

A notice dated 1821 gives details of the Mersey & Irwell Company's carrying activities, and incorporates a packet-boat timetable. Note the reference to the "newly-erected Wet Dock, Old Quay, Liverpool," and the fact that vessels with cargoes to tranship are admitted free of charge into the company's docks. Note also that the packet-boat fares are identical with those charged on the Bridgewater Canal.

A poster of 1837 offers moral advice to Bridgewater boatmen.

## Mersey and Irwell Navigation.

*Office at the Old Quay, Water-street*—Thomas Ogden Lingard, *principal agent—Receiving House, 1 Meal street.*

By this conveyance goods are forwarded daily to and from Liverpool, Runcorn, Warrington and Manchester, and from thence, by canal or land carriage, to all intermediate and adjacent places.

This Company possess very spacious and commodious docks at Runcorn, about sixteen miles above Liverpool, on the course of the Mersey towards Manchester, which afford great accommodation and advantages to the Irish traders and coasting vessels generally.

Particular attention is given to the discharging of vessels, and their cargoes may be trans-shipped into lighters and their vessels, and immediately forwarded into the interior of the country, forming a convenient intercourse with the commercial and agricultural districts of Lancashire, Cheshire, Yorkshire, and the adjacent country.—A very commodious slip is formed in the pier for the landing of cattle and carriages, and for the accommodation of the steam packets.

For the convenience of the Irish and Scotch trade, arrangements are made for sending vessels direct to the Clarence Dock, Liverpool.—An allowance is made upon all goods for Liverpool delivered at the Quay.—All goods delivered after the hours stated in the time table will not be considered in time for the ensuing tide; and the carters must not on any account stop to take in loading afterwards, *if they have other goods* in their carts, as in several instances have nearly missed their passage by the carts being so detained.

Agent at Liverpool.......William Guyten.
Agent at Warrington.......James Dawson.
Agent at Runcorn.........Edward Atherton Lingard.

NEW QUAY COMPANY, daily carriers by water to and from Liverpool, 126 Water street, Bridge street, Manchester; and Parade wharf, Liverpool.—Joseph Willoughby, agent.

## Passage Boats from the New Bailey.

Elegant and commodious Packet Boats, for passengers and their luggage, sail every morning to and from Manchester, Warrington and Runcorn; and there is a commodious Steam Packet at Runcorn, which meets the Company's Packets for the conveyance of passengers, &c. to and from Liverpool.

Extra Packets, during the summer season, also sail every day about six hours before high water at Liverpool, by which passengers may go through direct to Liverpool in seven hours. The time of sailing, and other particulars, may be known by cards, to be had at the OLD QUAY OFFICE; or at Messrs. Bancks and Co.'s Exchange-street; the Albion Hotel, Piccadilly; or at the Old Quay, and Sugar Loaves Taverns, Water street, Manchester.

Further particulars, with Tables of the departure of the boats, fares, &c. may be had on application at the MERSEY and IRWELL NAVIGATION OFFICE, Old Quay, Manchester.

## Warrington, Runcorn, &c. Passage Boats, from Castle Quay.

Two elegant Passage Boats, George Hitchmough and Matthew Fyes, *masters*, (for passengers and their luggage only,) go alternately from Manchester to Runcorn; one of which leaves Castle Quay, Knott mill, Manchester, every morning at eight; passes Altrincham at ten; London Boat, near Warrington, at one; passes Preston Brook, near Frodsham, at two; and arrives at Runcorn, at three (except Saturday), when it leaves Manchester at ten, and is correspondently later at the above named places. One leaves Runcorn every morning at nine; arrives at Preston Brook at ten; passes London Bridge at twelve; Altrincham at half-past two; and arrives at Castle Quay, Manchester, every afternoon at half-past four.

Another Passage Boat, William Morris, *master*, sets off from Lymm, every morning at six, passes Altrincham at half-past seven, and arrives at Manchester at half-past nine; it returns the same evening, at four in the winter season, and at five in the summer.

Also an extra Passage Boat, from Manchester to Altrincham, every day at one (Sunday excepted), when it leaves at eight in the morning, and returns from Altrincham in winter at four, and in summer at six.

Extra Packets, during the summer season, sail every day, from the Castle Quay, Manchester, for Liverpool; the passage through being made in seven hours; the times of starting are regulated by the tide.—The particulars of which may be known by applying at the Duke's warehouse, or the Flower Pot, Knott mill.

| FARES. | Front Room. | | Back Room. | |
|---|---|---|---|---|
| | s. | d. | s. | d. |
| To Stretford | 0 | 6 | 0 | 4 |
| To Altrincham | 0 | 9 | 0 | 6 |
| To Dunham | 1 | 0 | 0 | 8 |
| To Lymm | 1 | 6 | 1 | 0 |
| To London Bridge | 2 | 0 | 1 | 3 |
| To Preston Brook | 2 | 6 | 1 | 6 |
| To Runcorn | 3 | 0 | 2 | 0 |

## Worsley Passage Boats.

A passage Boat, Edmund Simister, *master*, leaves Worsley at half-past seven in the morning, and arrives at Manchester at half-past nine; returns at ten, arrives at Worsley at twelve; leaves Worsley at half-past two in winter, and three in summer; arrives in Manchester at half-past four in winter, and five in summer; leaves Manchester at five in winter, and six in summer, and arrives at Worsley at seven in winter, and eight in summer.

| FARES. | Front Room. | | Back Room. | |
|---|---|---|---|---|
| | s. | d. | s. | d. |
| To Barton | 0 | 6 | 0 | 4 |
| To Worsley | 0 | 9 | 0 | 6 |
| To Astley | 1 | 2 | 0 | 9 |

## Wigan and Southport Passage Boat.

From the Duke's Quay, a Boat to Southport and Wigan every morning at eight (Sunday excepted).—Parcels, &c. to be left at Samuel Hague's, Packet house, 287 Deansgate.

| FARES. | Front Room. | | Back Room. | |
|---|---|---|---|---|
| | s. | d. | s. | d. |
| To Barton | 0 | 10 | 0 | 6 |
| To Worsley | 1 | 4 | 0 | 8 |
| To Astley | 1 | 8 | 1 | 0 |
| To Leigh | 1 | 10 | 1 | 3 |
| To Wigan | 2 | 6 | 1 | 9 |
| To Scarisbrick | 4 | 0 | 2 | 6 |

Children above two, and under seven years of age, half fare.

The 1841 Directory advertisements for the Mersey & Irwell Navigation and the Bridgewater Canal packet-boats both indicate that the starting time for the additional journeys in the summer season is influenced by the state of the tide on the Mersey, when the prompt connection with the Steam Packet at Runcorn would give a journey time of seven hours between Manchester and Liverpool on each system. Fares had been reduced to meet railway competition. The river navigation advertisement also gives details of their transhipment activities at Runcorn Docks.

of the Duke's canal, whereas the Company's boat came to anchor alongside their packet boat. However, he noted that this obvious convenience was outweighed by the delay and trouble in negotiating the locks on the river navigation, and complained that the views were often shut out by high and winding muddy banks. The second-class fare from Manchester to Liverpool was then two shillings (10p), but as the railways became established, their greater speed and convenience gradually captured the passenger traffic from the waterways, and, despite a drastic fare reduction, the packet-boats ceased in the 1860s.

In 1825, a company organised by Matthew Hedley, a Manchester grocer, made application for Parliamentary permission to cut a 45-mile 'ship canal' from the estuary of the River Dee through Lymm and Altrincham to Didsbury, in South Manchester. The application was rejected because plans had not been deposited, but the reaction of Liverpool gave a taste of things to come. A poem appeared in the Liverpool press, relating how Neptune, the God of the Sea, had become lost, and by mistake had swum up the 'ship canal' to Manchester. Meeting a crowd of Mancunians, he:–

"Advised them in future to stick to their Jennies,
And in aping their betters, not make themselves ninnies."

Although the scheme was unsuccessful, it attracted a great deal of publicity, and a song, lamenting the fact that the project had not been taken up, was performed in a Manchester theatre in 1825–26, and afterwards its words were printed and circulated. It began:–

"I sing a theme deserving praise,
A theme of great renown, sir,
The Ship Canal in Manchester,
That rich and trading town, sir."

Another verse forecast the decline of Liverpool if the 'ship canal' scheme was implemented:–

"Alas, too, for poor Liverpool,
She'd surely go to pot, sir,
For want of trade, her folks would starve,
Her Custom House would rot, sir.
I'm wrong, they'd not exactly starve
Or want, for it is true, sir,
They might come down to Manchester,
We'd find 'em work to do, sir."

The boat steps (left) by the Packet House at Worsley were the calling point for passenger services on the Bridgewater Canal. The main line of the canal passes from left to right across the picture. The branch (centre right) leads through the bridge to Worsley Delph and the entrance to the mines' underground canals. The vessel in the foreground is one of the large barges, and moored beyond are some of the 'starvationers,' so called because of their narrow construction, essential in the restricted underground system, from which they brought coal in iron or wooden containers.

The opening of the Liverpool & Manchester Railway in 1830 saw no immediate diminution of trade on either the Mersey & Irwell river navigation or the Bridgewater Canal, though competition continued in the form of toll reductions and waiving of lockage charges for the independent carriers, and offers of better services. The Bridgewater undertaking enjoyed the advantages of connections to a network of other canals — the Rochdale Canal (at Castlefield, Manchester), the Leeds & Liverpool Canal (at Leigh), and the Trent & Mersey Canal (at Preston Brook) — all of which brought increased traffic and profits. The Mersey & Irwell Navigation was connected with the Manchester, Bolton & Bury Canal in 1808 by means of a flight of six locks located between the River Irwell and the Oldfield Road canal wharves in Salford. An idea of 1801 was revived by the Mersey & Irwell Company in 1835, when, jointly with the Manchester, Bolton & Bury Canal Company, it proposed a navigable tunnel to connect the Irwell with the Rochdale Canal. Circumstances were favourable at that date because of the vast tonnage of goods being carted overland between the two systems, and authority was gained in an Act of 1836. The Company invested a great deal of money and effort into this joint venture, the 'Manchester & Salford Junction Canal,' which opened in 1839. Although less than a mile long, the difference in water level between the two systems required five locks, and the tunnel under the city centre caused considerable difficulties. The entrance lock from the Irwell was on the Manchester side, almost opposite the entrance to the Bury and Bolton Canal, on a site now occupied by Granada Television studios. The Junction Canal emerged to join an arm of the Rochdale Canal near the present G-Mex Exhibition Centre on Lower Mosley Street. Unhappily, it proved a commercial failure, returns never justifying the great expense of construction. The Salford Junction Act of 1836 had also empowered the Bridgewater Canal Company to make their own connection with the Irwell at Hulme, near Regent Bridge. This was done in 1838 and provided a much easier means of access to the Rochdale Canal than the difficult and expensively-operated Junction Canal. As early as 1841, the Junction Canal was offered to the Mersey & Irwell Company free of charge, the latter, fearing that otherwise it would be closed, agreeing to take over full responsibility for its operation.

Prospects seemed happier on other parts of the Mersey & Irwell waterway. The tonnage carried was increasing year by year, but in 1837 Warrington businessmen asked Sir John Rennie, a leading canal engineer, to investigate the idea of building a barrage with locks across the narrow part of the Mersey estuary near Runcorn. Rennie's

Steam tugs were used to tow canal barges across the Mersey estuary between Runcorn and Liverpool. The 'Earl Of Ellesmere,' built for the Bridgewater undertaking in 1857, is seen moored by the wharf at Runcorn. This tug and eight others, built in the period 1857–1877, eventually passed into the ownership of the Ship Canal Company, becoming the nucleus of the tugboat fleet which guided ships to Manchester. The Ship Canal Company also adopted the Bridgewater funnel markings of two white bands set on a black background.

report was published in 1838, reviving the idea of a canal large enough to be used by ocean-going ships. He argued that a channel dredged from Runcorn to Warrington could eventually be extended to Manchester, with locks where necessary, and that this would be preferable to improving the river navigation.

Traders complained bitterly about the expensive rates (allegedly exhorbitant) demanded by Liverpool for organising the flow of commerce through that city. Vessels using Liverpool to tranship goods to or from Manchester had to pay dock charges and, in addition, dues were levied on all merchandise passing through the port. If it were possible for ocean-going ships to sail directly to Manchester, these costs (and rail charges, if goods were moved overland) would be avoided. A secondary source of irritation for Manchester's civic leaders was the belief that only a small proportion of Liverpool's port dues was spent on providing dock facilities. The rest was spent on improving the town, a policy which Manchester considered selfish.

In 1840 two 'ship canal' schemes were published. One, by H.R.Palmer, Vice-President of the Institute of Civil Engineers, sought to enlarge the Mersey & Irwell Navigation by making deeper and wider cuts, with larger locks. The other, by John Bateman, would have constructed an embankment across the Mersey to give deep water as far as Warrington. Unhappily, this was the period of 'railway mania' when energy and funds throughout the country were concentrated on the spread of the iron roads. The river company, with only limited funds to spare, tried to secure a share of the railway traffic by deepening the Irwell between their Water Street wharves and Victoria Bridge, Manchester. By enabling 'flats' to go further upstream, close to the terminus of the Manchester & Leeds Railway, it was hoped that the transfer of cargoes from barges to wagons, and vice-versa, would be facilitated, and would enable the Company to handle Yorkshire imports and exports. Instead, the Manchester & Leeds Railway Company chose to link up with the Manchester & Liverpool Railway. However, the clearance of this stretch of waterway enabled the pleasure boats to embark passengers further upstream, in front of Manchester Cathedral.

On the 20th October 1840, there took place an interesting demonstration of the possibilities lying ahead. The cargo ship 'Mary,' albeit a small vessel, arrived via the river navigation direct from Dublin with a cargo of potatoes, discharging at the Old Quay Company's wharf near Victoria Bridge. The 'Mary' then proceeded to take on a cargo of coal from a Pendleton colliery as the return consignment to Dublin. The arrival of the 'Mary' was considered to be prophetic, and a poem, published in honour of the occasion, included the lines:–

> And soon may scores of others
> Perform the trip with her,
> And trade and commerce double
> In noble Manchester.

Two strings of barges towed by one steam tug are seen in the Mersey estuary, crossing from Runcorn to Liverpool. Runcorn and the Wirral shoreline are seen in the background. The leading barge on the right is named 'Bertie Abbott,' whilst the rearmost vessel appears to be a conversion from a masted ship.

But the sad fact was that the Mersey & Irwell Company was suffering badly as a result of competition from the railways and the Bridgewater Canal. Rates had been forced down. The river company was desperately short of funds, and quite unable to invest in any further improvements. The Bridgewater Canal, managed by Trustees since the Duke's death in 1803, was prosperous, but its operators knew that if the river navigation could be enlarged to admit the passage of ocean-going ships, then canal revenue would suffer. Consequently, the Bridgewater Trustees determined to buy-out their old rivals at a cost of £402,000, becoming the owners of both waterways in 1844. The merger effectively put an end to the old river company's scheme for a ship canal. Independent boat-owners continued to use the river navigation, and took over the cargoes formerly carried by Company craft, but the Bridgewater Trustees met railway competition by concentrating on canal improvements, regarding the river system merely as a stand-by in case of need. An ambitious proposal of 1845 by James Acland came to nothing, but from this date, whenever railway companies wished to construct lines across the Mersey & Irwell route, the owners of the waterway insisted on the inclusion of a clause in the Parliamentary Act providing that, if a ship canal was ever built, the rail bridges must be converted to swing bridges to allow ships to pass. In the meantime, dredging was neglected, and the rivers silted up, causing floods in wet weather. Concern about the deterioration of the river system was expressed in 1852, when the passenger boat 'Jack Sharp,' built specially for the river route in 1838, was withdrawn from service because it could no longer operate satisfactorily between Warrington and Manchester due to lack of draught. By that date, passenger traffic was negligible on the river, and the Bridgewater packet boats had suffered a decline after the opening of the railway to Altrincham.

On the river, floods brought different dangers, and it was recorded that in times of spate, tow-horses were sometimes drowned when 'flats' sailing on fast currents, pulled their horses from the tow-paths into the river. The worst flood occurred on the 13th November 1866, when, after three days of heavy rain, the Irwell rose 14 feet above its normal level. After each flood, more mudbanks appeared in the shallows and locks were blocked with silt, making it difficult for the boats to reach Manchester. In 1840 vessels with a draught of 5 feet 4 inches had successfully negotiated the rivers, but by 1860 even boats drawing only 3½ feet were having difficulty, and there were many periods when an insufficient depth of water made passage completely impracticable.

Users of the river navigation had to contend with droughts, shallows, and floods. The Bridgewater system had none of those drawbacks, but traffic was sometimes halted when the canal froze over. The barges seen here are stuck fast in the ice at Oughtrington, near Lymm, Cheshire.

In an attempt to maintain freedom of movement on the canal in freezing conditions, teams of ice-breakers were employed. By rocking their boat from side to side, the men tried to break up the ice to make a channel of clear water. On one occasion, the towing horse bolted, causing the boat and its human cargo to ride up over the ice, on which it slid along at alarming speed.

The Bridgewater Canal, however, remained a keen competitor for the railways. It carried bulk cargoes at a cheaper rate, and was almost as quick, so it was inevitable that a group of railway companies sought to assume management of the canal. In 1871 Parliament condemned a projected take-over, for there was an outcry against the continued absorption of canals by the railway companies. But just one year later, the Bridgewater Navigation Company, was formed to acquire both the canal and the river navigation system, together with all associated vessels, buildings, and dock installations. The new company, consisting almost entirely of railway shareholders, paid £1,120,000 to place the waterways under railway control. Edward Leader Williams, Jnr., engineer to the Weaver Navigation since 1856, was appointed to be General Manager and Engineer of the Bridgewater Navigation Company. Leader Williams had effected considerable improvements to the Weaver Navigation, including widening work, new cuts to avoid bends, better locks and sluices, and from 1865 enlargement of the Weaver Docks at Weston Point to admit sea-going vessels. He was also anxious to make a connection between the Weaver and the Trent & Mersey Canal at Anderton, and in 1872 gained authority to construct his famous 'boat lift.' Leader Williams moved to the Bridgewater undertaking in 1872 before the boat lift was completed, but remained as consultant until the lift opened in 1875.

In 1872 Leader Williams' appointment to the Bridgewater Navigation Company led to the purchase of a fleet of steam tugs for use on the canal. Steam tugs had previously been used only in the open water of the Mersey estuary. Those intended for use on the canal were of smaller dimensions, and eventually numbered twenty-seven, all named after places in Lancashire or Cheshire. Tug 'Stalybridge' is towing a line of heavy barges by Walton Hall, Cheshire.

The steam tugs were not immune from freezing fast into the ice when conditions were severe. Tug 'Todmorden' waits to be freed by the ice-breakers.

Despite the controlling interests of the railway companies, Leader Williams in his new post made improvements to the Bridgewater system and invested in a fleet of narrow-beam steam tugs to increase efficiency on the canal. Five steam tugs were in use by the end of 1874, and the fleet numbered 26 by 1881.

The Mersey & Irwell river navigation, however, was regarded merely as a secondary system, useful only on occasions when stoppages or repairs were necessary on the canal. The steam tugs were found to cause erosion on the Bridgewater Canal, which diverted funds for urgent deepening and re-walling of most lengths. Consequently, funds for improvement being unavailable, the river system was allowed to decline still further. In 1876 George Hicks, of the Manchester Chamber of Commerce, having seen boats stuck fast on the mud of the Irwell, wrote a letter to the 'Manchester Guardian' suggesting a 'ship canal' in preference to the use of the railways. Hicks' letter prompted Hamilton Fulton, a London engineer, to submit a scheme in 1877, but no action resulted. The neglected state of the rivers drew protests from the small carrying firms who still wished to use them, and also from Manchester councillors, who accused the Bridgewater Company of acting against the public interest in deliberately allowing the river navigation to fall into disuse.

This sad state of affairs was exacerbated when, in the late 1870s, the world-wide trade depression saw Manchester grappling with the alarming symptoms of economic stagnation. Industries failed, mills and workshops emptied, shops closed, and there was a steady migration away from the city. It became known that a major engineering firm, the locomotive-builders Sharp, Stewart & Company, was about to move from Manchester to the banks of the Clyde in order to secure cheaper carriage. Leading businessmen realised that lower transport costs were vital to the region's survival as a commercial centre, but debated how to tackle the two main, related problems. These were, firstly, that the port of Liverpool, in its own interests, was charging what Manchester men considered to be excessively high rates for its services in importing raw cotton, and, secondly, that the railway companies were taking advantage of their monopoly to charge high rates for the transport of goods to and from the cotton

Steam tugs did not completely replace animal-power for towage, and there were still many horses to be seen on the tow-paths. A notice of 1873 warns boatmen about the proper care of their charges.

Barges 'Lizzie Bate' and 'Edna Bate' at the Castlefield wharves in Manchester, terminus of the Bridgewater Canal.

towns. This handicap was exemplified by the fact that Oldham spinners could buy cotton in Germany or France, pay the costs of importing via Hull, add railway charges from across the Pennines, and still make a saving on the price they would have paid for the same cotton in Liverpool. On the export side, over half the cost of sending a ton of cotton goods to India was absorbed in railway and dock charges at Liverpool. There was a need for Manchester exports to be cheaper and more competitive — it was claimed that it cost more to send goods from Manchester to Liverpool than from London to Bombay.

Consequently, the advantages of a deep, wide waterway from Manchester to the sea became uppermost once more in

Daniel Adamson

the minds of the region's traders. George Hicks and Hamilton Fulton managed to interest several businessmen in the idea of a tidal 'ship canal', and in April 1881 the members of the Manchester Chamber of Commerce considered this proposal, and passed a resolution in support of a waterway. Much public debate followed, and on the 27th June 1882 the historic meeting, which proved to be the first formal step in the Ship Canal project, took place at the Didsbury home of Daniel Adamson.

Adamson, who had an engineering business in Dukinfield, had invited civic representatives of thirteen large Lancashire towns, together with fifty-five merchants and manufacturers, "to consider the practicability of constructing a tidal waterway to Manchester, and to take such action thereon as may be determined." Those present had before them the information that four-

"The Port Of Manchester In 1950" was a cartoon which appeared in "Tit-Bits" in 1883. It depicts a thriving Manchester some 70 years on after becoming a port, and a declining Liverpool, the inhabitants of the latter city leaving to seek employment inland.

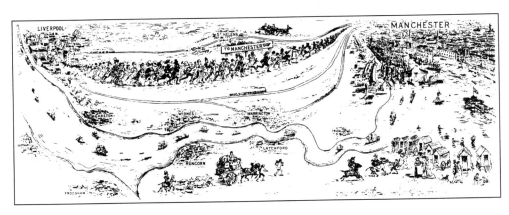

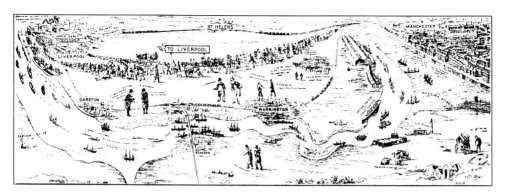

A response to the "Tit-Bits" cartoon was drawn by Liverpool artist W.T.Gray. Basing his work on the original cartoon, he depicted the situation as it might be in 1960, with Manchester failing, ships aground, premises empty, and movement of population back towards Liverpool.

fifths of the export trade of Liverpool passed through Manchester. A Provisional Committee was formed, with authority to commission a detailed survey of the route of a possible waterway, and to take any necessary steps to form the 'Manchester Tidal Navigation Company.'

Hamilton Fulton and Leader Williams, the latter by then an independent consultant, though retained by the Bridgewater Company, were each invited to prepare a report on a scheme for a tidal navigation. Both recommended that a deeply-dredged channel, retained by stone walls, should be constructed in the middle of the Mersey estuary as far as Warrington. From that point, Fulton's plan was similar to his 1877 proposal, by which a channel without locks would be excavated so as to allow tides to reach Manchester. This would have placed the terminal docks at the bottom of a deep excavation, as Manchester lies some sixty feet above sea-level. Leader Williams submitted a plan for deepening and widening the old Mersey & Irwell Navigation, taking the tide over half way, after which there would be a succession of locks. Road and rail bridges would be raised or made to swing, whilst the Bridgewater Canal difficulty could be solved by a boat lift on each side, similar to the Anderton boat lift he had already installed on the Weaver Navigation. The Leader Williams proposal was deemed to be the most feasible, and there followed a series of public meetings to rouse support for the project and to raise funds for the necessary Parliamentary Bill. The proponents found themselves up against extraordinary opposition, and not only from the vested interests of Liverpool and the railway companies. Even the 'Manchester Guardian' was lukewarm, noting that "real salt water could not come to Manchester." The criticism, hostility, and lack of enthusiasm halted the in-flow of funds.

Supporters of the project tried to restore confidence. They argued that there was little point in Lancashire industry producing cheap goods, if they could not be transported at cheap rates. Those who claimed that a ship canal would not pay, were reminded that the same objection had been raised a century before against the Bridgewater Canal and fifty years ago against the Liverpool & Manchester Railway. So great was the tonnage of goods handled by the docks at Liverpool, that if Manchester secured only a proportion of that traffic, a ship canal would be a profitable investment. Ferdinand de Lesseps, of Suez Canal fame, was brought to speak at the Free Trade Hall, and numerous pamphlets extolled the benefits to be gained from a ship canal to Manchester. Such a waterway was

*Edward Leader Williams*

29

said to be essential to "break the tyranny of railway company 'rings.'" The Chairman of the London & North Western Railway unwittingly played into the hands of the promoters when, in his half-yearly statement, he admitted that "the sea and canals do more to bring down railway rates than any competition amongst the railways themselves."

The Bridgewater Navigation Company prepared its argument in opposition to any proposal for a Ship Canal, and intended to demonstrate that the river navigation was not being neglected. Indeed, in 1879, when the Bridgewater Canal was closed for six days for annual maintenance work, no fewer than 269 'flats' used the Mersey & Irwell system. But critics alleged that in 1878 the river navigation was able to be used by 50-ton boats for only 201 working days. In 1880 that figure had dropped to 110, in 1881 to 50, in 1882 to 47, and in 1883 to 32. In the month of October of that year, the

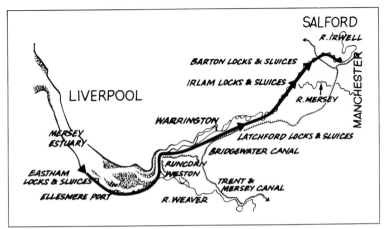

The first plans submitted for the Ship Canal were based on the use of channels and training walls in the Mersey estuary as far as Runcorn. After two unsuccessful applications, a third scheme gained Parliamentary approval in 1885. The main difference was the incorporation of an extended cutting along the southern shore of the estuary, separated from the tidal channel by an embankment, and with entrance locks at Eastham.

river was not usable for a single day. The Company Engineer produced statistics to show that more dredging was being carried out in the early 1880s than ever before, and that funds were devoted to improvements to locks and weirs, including in 1882 a new tilting weir at Throstles Nest. (A 'tilting weir' consisted of panels which were held upright when it was necessary to keep a good depth of water upstream, but which could be angled, or tilted, when required to allow debris, silt or flood water to move away quickly downstream.) The Engineer's figures disguised the fact that the heavily used portions of the waterway were restricted to the Runcorn and Latchford Canal, and the length above Throstles Nest Lock, the latter being used by river traffic joining the Bridgewater Canal via Hulme Locks. Therefore, maintenance and dredging were concentrated in these two lengths, whilst the centre part of the river navigation was little used, and virtually closed to through traffic by 1883 by virtue of the accumulation of debris and silt.

Even so, to combat the Ship Canal plans, a scheme was drawn up for enlarging existing locks from 70 by 15½ feet to 154 by 32 feet, with a minimum draught of 10 feet. (Ten years on, the Ship Canal locks were 600 by 65 feet, with a depth of 26 feet.) It was also planned to deepen and widen the Runcorn and Latchford Canal, and to replace all weirs with the tilting type as at Throstles Nest. Two weirs (at Warrington and Mode Wheel) were, indeed, replaced with the new type, and a new channel, the New Barns Cut, was made at Mode Wheel, but other works were dependent upon the failure of the Ship Canal project. Had the Ship Canal plan failed, the way would have been clear for the Company's own improvement scheme.

The first two bills submitted to Parliament for the construction of the Ship Canal were rejected. Principal objectors included the Bridgewater Navigation Company, the railway companies, and the Mersey Docks & Harbour Board. After lengthy examination in the Commons, the first bill was rejected by a five-man Lords' committee in August 1883 because it was deemed "not expedient" to proceed in that session. A newspaper editorial described the procedure as a "monstrous and most expensive farce." A second application was made in the next session. In May 1884 the Lords passed the Bill subject to the proviso that work should not

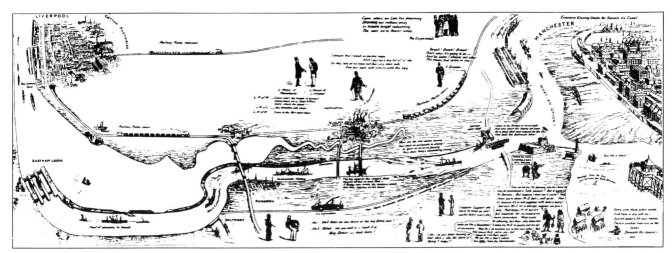

Another attempt to "ridicule the canal out of existence" (Bosdin Leech) was this second cartoon by W.T.Gray, based on the third 'Ship Canal' scheme with entrance locks at Eastham. The artist sought to show assorted dangers on the proposed navigation and the ruination of businessmen who invested money in the project. Other Liverpool-based propaganda against the Ship Canal project ranged from music hall songs and pantomime references to reasoned economic argument.

commence until £5,000,000 had been subscribed, but a Select Committee of the Commons rejected the Bill, influenced in their decision by the promise of Liverpool interests not to oppose a new Bill which would request powers to construct a canal along the shore of the estuary, instead of in the middle.

To attract subscribers to the Parliamentary Fund, coupons costing one shilling (5p) each could be purchased. When ten or more had been collected, the holder could apply for priority in the first share issue.

The cheque for the purchase of the Bridgewater Navigation Company, dated 3rd August 1887, was the highest amount ever presented up to that date. The purchase price of £1,700,000 had been fixed by Act of Parliament.

When the third Bill was submitted, the Bridgewater Navigation Company announced that it did not wish to sell the canal and the river navigation to the promoters. Instead, the Company wished to carry out its own scheme for the improvement of the river navigation, and to introduce steam tugs to tow large barges. However, when the Manchester Ship Canal Act received assent in August 1885, it included a clause which stated that the Bridgewater undertaking, which included the river navigation, must be purchased, and that the Bridgewater Canal must be kept in good order and open for navigation for all who wished to use it. The new Act incorporated several alterations to the previous scheme, substituting an entrance lock at Eastham and a land cutting with embankment or training walls for ten miles along the Cheshire side of the estuary. The changes effectively dealt with Liverpool's main objections and at the same time placed the entrance lock conveniently outside the range of Liverpool port dues.

Even with the passing of the third Bill, cynicism remained. A comic poem entitled 'The Manchester Ship Canal,' published in 1885 (the author being identified only by the initials 'R.S.K.'), had as its theme a ship's stormy voyage along the proposed waterway. The last two verses read:–

> "Close reef the sails," the bosun cried, "we're in a great dilemma.
> Just row her to Pomona Bay, she cannot stand the weather.
> She's sprung a leak, now all is lost, let each man do his best,
> For soon she'll be a total wreck on the shoals of Throstles' Nest."
> But soon the storm abated, it was rather over-rated,
> When captain, crew and officers were quickly congregated.
> They searched the chart in every part to find their situation,
> They were east-north-east of Bailey Bridge, just south of Salford Station."

After the successful passage of the Bill, it remained necessary to raise £5,000,000 before work could commence. An additional £1,710,000 was required for the purchase of the Bridgewater Navigation Company. Unfortunately, money was not forthcoming. There appeared to be a serious difference of opinion between most of the directors and Daniel Adamson, who was resolutely opposed to the idea of a Lancashire enterprise being financed by London sources. Confidence in the project seemed lacking, and a committee of independent businessmen was set up to pronounce on the soundness of the scheme. They recommended a strengthening of the Board, as a result of which Daniel Adamson resigned from his position as Chairman, to be replaced by Lord Egerton of Tatton. Fund-raising improved, and by July 1887 the Bridgewater canal and river systems were purchased by the presentation of a cheque for £1,710,000, the largest cheque ever written up to that time. In August 1887 it was announced that the necessary £5,000,000 had been raised, and that work would be allowed to start.

# THE CONSTRUCTION PERIOD, 1887–1893.

Over five years elapsed between Daniel Adamson's 1882 meeting and the commencement of work on the Ship Canal on the 11th November 1887. The enabling Act was passed in June 1885, Parliamentary approval having cost over half-a-million pounds. The Duke of Bridgewater's earlier struggles had established the principle that public transport requirements should take precedence over the rights of individual land-owners. Now, negotiations and valuations took up much time. When the necessary funds were assured and the first land had been purchased, Thomas Andrew Walker was appointed contractor for the project. Lord Egerton, Chairman, ceremonially cut the first sod at a spot some three-quarters of a mile from Eastham, and Leader Williams, Engineer-in-Chief, wheeled away the first barrow-load of soil. Thomas Walker, then aged 60, was known to be a considerate employer. His previous experience included railway construction at home and abroad. Between 1865 and 1871 he had managed the construction of the Metropolitan and District Underground Railways in London, as a result of which the Great Western Railway had appointed him to finish the Severn Tunnel. He estimated that the Ship Canal would take $4\frac{1}{2}$ years to complete. The 36-mile route was divided into nine (later reduced to eight) sections, with an engineer in charge of each, and, pending the acquisition of further land, work began at four points, Eastham, Warrington, Warburton, and Salford. Walker's first task was to assemble equipment and materials, and engage a labour force. The site selected for the main terminal docks, near Trafford Bridge, Salford, on land purchased from Lord Egerton, shows an early stage in the collection of contractor's plant. The old river, on the left, was used to convey materials.

*Thomas Andrew Walker*

The contractor provided hundreds of miles of temporary railway track along the projected route, on which to distribute materials and carry away the excavated rock and soil. The Ashbury Company of Manchester undertook to deliver 100 wagons per week for the next twelve months. A line all the way from Eastham to Manchester was completed very quickly, and a supply train ran the full length each day. The scene at Barton shows a train of spoil wagons being hauled along track on the south bank of the Irwell. The view is looking upstream, towards Salford, with Brindley's stone aqueduct hidden behind the road bridge. St.Catherine's Church spire is to the right, with that of All Saints' Chapel beyond.

An early view of excavations near Frodsham Marsh. Loaded wagons wait to be hauled away on track laid on the base of the cut. December 1887 saw the first steam navvy in use, for Walker was anxious to supplement manual labour in every way possible. Rockspoil removed from the excavations at the western end of the Canal was dumped upon the Pool Hall Rocks, where it was available for ballast. It gradually grew in height until it became 'Mount Manisty.' Mr. Manisty was the Contractor's Agent for the No. 1 Section, and he and his wife were highly regarded by the labour force, not least for their philanthropic work and their organisation of entertainments around Eastham. It was fitting that the huge mountain of earth should be named after him.

Mechanical excavators were soon in use along the length of the workings, but could not replace the spade and the wheelbarrow entirely. Navvies wielding shovels load wagons near Acton Grange. Walker built whole villages to house the navvies, and provided mission rooms (with resident chaplains) and other amenities. The navvies were itinerant workers, who moved from one large undertaking to another. Although they had a reputation for being rough and uncivilised, they proved hard-working and resilient in face of adverse weather and primitive living conditions. They earned about 4½d per hour, and with a 10-hour day, the weekly wage totalled between £1 and £1 5s (£1.25). At peak, over 16,000 labourers were employed on the Ship Canal project, together with specialist craftsmen, such as stonemasons, carpenters, bricklayers, machinery operators, engine drivers, etc.

Section No.1 ran from Eastham to Ellesmere Port, and included the embankments along the tidal estuary. The section beyond, which included the Runcorn docks, had to be left untouched for the time being, as its links with the Mersey estuary had to be kept open to enable ships to reach the port until it was possible to use the completed western sections of the new canal. Eastham lay 19 miles from the Mersey Bar. In this view, work on the entrance locks is well-advanced, and excavations to deepen the approach channel are under way at low water. The outside channel was excavated to such a depth as would allow access at any state of the tide, but as bigger ships came into use, times of entering the canal were regulated.

A 'navvy bucket' in use at Weaste on the section near Mode Wheel. Temporary railway track was laid at the base of excavations, and moved about as work progressed and the channel deepened. In this case, a horse is being used to marshal loaded wagons into trains, to be hauled away by a steam locomotive.

A 'French Navvy' land dredger at work near Mode Wheel. Its buckets worked round an endless chain, scooping and depositing the spoil direct into railway wagons. These large excavators were suitable for use only where the soil was soft, for they could not cope with rock or hard clay. Running on track at the side of the cut, they worked backwards and forwards along an excavation, gradually widening it as the rails were moved outwards. Their great weight sometimes caused the banks to collapse. Note that the railway track has a third rail to carry this broad-gauge excavator.

Whereas the Bridgewater Canal system remained in use, the Mersey & Irwell river navigation was irrevocably destroyed in the process of straightening and deepening the route for the Ship Canal. A steam crane and excavator operates here at the base of the workings. These smaller machines had the advantage of being able to swivel and excavate sideways or in awkward corners. Top right may be noted the remains of the gates at Stickings Lock, near Davyhulme. The sides of the lock have been torn down in making the deeper excavation.

Mechanisation did not obviate the need for 'barrow runs,' and great quantities of spoil were moved by hand. The 'runs' were sloping plank-ways, up which loaded barrows or carts were hauled by rope. Sometimes, power was provided by a horse-gin at the top, a navvy guiding the barrow along the planks. At other times, man-power alone sufficed. A May 1889 view near Cadishead shows two such 'runs' in use. Note the mechanical excavator working at yet a lower level, and the evidence left by the sleepers of recently-removed rail track.

Another barrow-road incline close to the Irlam railway viaduct appears to have been equipped with light-section portable rails. Note what seems to be a brick-making mould in the centre foreground, though the contractor set up a 'brick farm' at Thelwall, which produced 70 million bricks.

During the period of construction of the Ship Canal, there were over 6000 wagons in use, together with some 180 steam locomotives, working on over 200 miles of temporary track. Some of the locomotives were built specially for the Ship Canal contract, others were brought from projects elsewhere. The 'Raglan' had been built in 1887 by the Hunslet Engine Company for T.A.Walker. On completion of the contract, it was retained by the Ship Canal Company.

Thomas Walker died on the 25th November 1889, aged 62. On the side of the railway gatekeeper's cabin at Thelwall is a notice of a special service to be held in his memory at the local mission hall. Walker had been regarded as a benevolent employer, to whom

his men were fiercely loyal. On such a contract, it was inevitable that some workers would suffer serious accidents, and a chain of first-aid stations and three base hospitals (temporary buildings of timber) had been strategically sited along the line of the canal. Any seriously-injured workmen were transported to the nearest hospital without delay on the contractor's railway. A Liverpool surgeon, Robert Jones, was appointed in 1888 to supervise what is thought to be the first organised accident service in the history of British surgery. Between 1888 and 1893 there were over 3000 major accidents, and the medical team also treated illnesses such as pneumonia and rheumatic fever. Walker continued to care for, and employ anyone injured in his service. Light duties were offered to disabled men, who became known as 'Walker's Fragments.' The workman on the ground, sitting on his pick, appears to be cleaning out the points. Note the water tower to replenish the steam locomotives.

Wherever there happens to be a large body of working men, services of one sort or another inevitably follow. A floating 'lodging house,' looking rather like Noah's Ark, is seen here moored in the estuary near Norton Marsh. It appears to be a conversion from an old river 'flat.' From his weekly wage of just over £1, it was estimated that a navvy would spend about 13s (65p) on food and lodging.

Also on hand to attend to the needs of the workers were various suppliers of food and drink. This drinks man and girl were photographed at Mode Wheel in 1890. His yoke supports two urns, probably containing tea and coffee, whilst the girl carries a basket full of cups and mugs.

Even a temporary contractor's railway had to make use of signalling arrangements at busy spots on the system. A primitive signal post at Mode Wheel carried six arms to control train movements. The young operator stands with his hand on the metal rods, with which he could pull the slotted post indicators. Note also the three lanterns, which could be rotated to guide movements after dark. The cabin bears the chalk notice, 'No Loafers Admitted,' an instruction repeated on the base of the lamp tower. The gantry behind the signals carries a travelling overhead crane for lifting and loading the stone blocks used in the construction of the lock sides and quays.

The contractor's railway was useful for transporting workers as well as materials. Work finished at mid-day on Saturdays, when the 'Saturday Mail' on the Ellesmere Port section was useful in carrying the men back to their villages. The open wagons have been fitted with removable frames as a safety measure, but that has not prevented one young man from hanging through the bars. The small boy on the left looks on in envy. After Walker's death, the Ship Canal Company itself took over the construction contract.

Because of the difficulty of moving large excavators between sites, certain equipment was assembled where needed. A land dredger is here under construction in Trafford Hall cutting in September 1890. The photograph was taken from Trafford Park, looking towards Weaste, the excavations being well-advanced. One of the small Wilson steam cranes sits on an adjoining track. Note the network of railway lines laid on the dry bed of the cutting. This was at a point where a new cut had been made to avoid a bend in the river.

The terminal docks at Salford as planned in 1888, showing the original course of the River Irwell. On the eastern side of Trafford Bridge, the Ship Canal and the Bridgewater Canal were, and remain, separated by only a few yards.

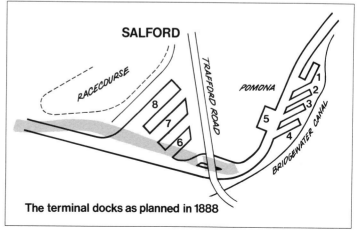

The terminal docks as planned in 1888

Along lengths of the canal where the earth was relatively soft, there was a danger that the banks would be eroded by the wash of passing ships. To prevent erosion, and to give more stability to the soil, a plaited matting of willow branches was fixed to the slopes. Dutch workmen were brought to give advice and teach the correct methods. This task was known as 'fascine work.' One length of the canal so treated was at Partington. When the water level of the canal was reduced temporarily in 1969, some of this work became visible for the first time since 1893, and was said to be as good as when first completed.

The western side of the Runcorn bridge was approached by a sharp curve. The embankment separating the canal from the estuary is on the left, with contractor's equipment on both banks. Some ten miles of embankment and sea-walls were necessary where the canal ran alongside the tideway and foreshore between Eastham and Runcorn. Over 13,000 piles were sunk to hold the embankments, which were faced with stone.

During construction, floods halted progress on several occasions, and sometimes ruined the work of many months. In January 1890, prolonged rain caused both the Mersey and the Irwell to overflow. Where the canal cut across the course of the old river, the ends of the excavations had been sealed by dams, but the rush of water was so great that the dams were washed away and the new sections were submerged prematurely. The subsequent pumping-out of the sections revealed damage to equipment. Overturned wagons are seen here at Flixton. Problems caused by the floods not only led to delays, but also cost more money than had been anticipated. Local authorities came to the rescue with generous loans to enable the project to be completed.

The first section of the canal ready for use was at the western end. A gap had been left in the embankment separating the canal from the Mersey estuary, providing a temporary entrance so that shipping movements to and from Ellesmere Port (terminus of the Shropshire Union Canal) would not be interrupted. This gap could not be closed until ships could reach the port via the canal. By mid-June 1891 the section was ready, and water was allowed in by making a hole in the dam and allowing the tide to spill over. Too sudden a rush of water might have damaged the banks, so the excavation was filled gradually over the course of a week, the level rising by about three feet with each tide. Engineers stand on the bank watching the first inrush of water. Further dredging, the removal of remaining obstacles, and some repair work where small earth slips had occurred, took place after the admission of water. Eastham Locks came into use on the 2nd July 1891.

Following the admittance of water to the western end of the canal, the gap which had been left in the embankment to give access to Ellesmere Port had to be closed. Train loads of ballast were tipped into the opening from both sides during the period of low water on the 11th July 1891, but the returning tide made a hole, and then completely broke down the new work. The photograph was taken after the failure of the first attempt. The great size of the gap may be judged from the scale of the figures standing in the centre of the opening. A second attempt was made the next day, this time using boulders, with heavy piles to stop them moving about, topped with clay and soil. This, too, failed, and the sea forced its way through. Engineers next decided to build up the embankment gradually with layers of concrete, and to raise the water level in the canal to equalise the pressure on each side. The third attempt began on the 14th July, when after 30 hours unceasing toil, the gap was finally closed. On the 16th July 1891 vessels began to use the Ship Canal to reach Ellesmere Port.

The completed entrance locks at Eastham consisted of three chambers, the largest (seen here) measuring 600 by 80 feet. A second lock, to the right, was 350 by 50 feet, and the third, intended only for barge traffic, 150 by 30 feet. When open at high tide, the minimum depth was 26 feet. The sluice gates are to the left. The main sea-lock is seen open to the estuary, with sailing vessels leaving as another waits to enter. As larger vessels came into use, it became the practice at Eastham for the Harbour Master's Department to control ship movement by allowing outward vessels to clear the locks in the four hours prior to high water. The deepest draught vessels would leave in the last few minutes when there would be maximum depth in the channel. Inward vessels would enter in the four hours after high water, when the ebb tide offered safer manoeuvring conditions, and when the berths at Eastham would be free to accommodate them. Largest vessels entered first. Smaller vessels could enter through the second lock most of the time.

The bridge which spanned the narrow estuary between Runcorn and Widnes had been constructed in 1866–68 by the London & North Western Railway Company, and had been designed to be sufficiently high to allow large ships to pass beneath if any should ever come that far up river. A clear headway of 75 feet had been stipulated, though, in fact, the Runcorn bridge was 84 feet above normal water level. When work began on the Ship Canal, the railway company opposed any deepening of the channel under the bridge, believing that such work might affect the foundations. The contractor drove piles into the river bed to support the embankment which separated the canal from the estuary. The section beneath the bridge was the narrowest part of the canal.

The upper portion of the canal was excavated for some 20 miles in as straight a course as possible. Rivers were intersected at no fewer than 30 points, so dams were left in place at the ends of each cutting, and channels were cut to pass off the river water. As each cutting was completed, the dams were excavated and dredged out, and rivers turned through the connected cuttings. One of the most advanced sections at the Manchester end of the canal in 1890 was the Little Bolton cutting, between Trafford Park and Weaste, which cut across to join a bend in the Irwell on the approach to the new Mode Wheel locks. When almost complete, and when only a few rails and tools remained to be cleared, the dam at the Mode Wheel end gave way after heavy rain, flooding the section prematurely. All the water had to be pumped out again on that occasion, but by mid-1891 the river water had been turned in, and the bucket dredger 'Irwell' was employed deepening this section and keeping the bottom free of silt and loose debris. The excavated material was loaded into tubs, seen on the barge alongside, and then moved by rail or tipped on to low land adjoining. On the far bank may be seen Irwell Bank House and, beyond, Ladywell Hospital.

By September 1891, 11 miles of the western end of the canal were in use. Originally, it had been intended to construct a large lock in the embankment to enable vessels to pass in from the Mersey, from where there had formerly been open access. However, to save the cost of constructing and maintaining a lock, ships of up to 400 tons were granted free use of the Canal as far as Ellesmere Port. Ships of a size that could not previously have entered the port, were required to pay a toll. It was claimed that Ellesmere Port now had a better entrance than before. Temporary docks at the mouth of the River Weaver were established for the import of grain and timber and the export of salt from Cheshire. A long landing stage was provided for this busy spot, ceremonially named 'Saltport' by the Chairman of the salt-exporters federation. The first foreign ship to use the Canal as far as Saltport was the Norwegian vessel 'Deodata,' which brought in Canadian timber and returned with a cargo of salt. Sailing ships are seen here at Saltport in July 1892.

By mid-1892 much of the excavation work on the upper reaches had been completed, and the terminal docks at Salford were nearly finished. An unusual feature was the construction of floating dredgers 'in the dry' at the bottom of completed cuttings. Such a one was the dredger 'Bollin,' built by Fleming & Fergusson of Paisley in the excavation between Warburton and Hollins Green. After water had been admitted to the section and the completed vessel floated, the dredger had to cut her own way out of the hollow in which she had been built. The same Company also built two more dredgers, the 'Irk' and the 'Medlock,' on the site of Salford Docks.

The Irlam Locks and sluices, seen here under construction, were completed in mid-1892. Apart from the three tidal locks at Eastham, the other locks (at Latchford, Irlam, Barton, and Mode Wheel) were built in pairs, the larger (on the left) measuring 600 by 65 feet, the smaller 350 by 45 feet. Between them, the four locks lifted vessels some 60 feet to Manchester's height above sea-level. The smaller lock was used for coastal vessels or barges, and was more economical in retaining water in the upper reaches of the canal. Both locks had to be used simultaneously if a large ship filled the main chamber completely. Then its accompanying tugs would be lifted in the small lock alongside. The sluice gates on the right could be raised or lowered to regulate the flow of water and maintain a constant level in the upper reaches of the canal.

At points where main roads crossed the course of the canal it was permissible to have swing bridges, but the same concession, though deemed suitable in the old 1845 scheme, was no longer applied to railway lines. Viaducts, approached by long and steady gradients, had to be constructed to raise the underside sufficiently high to allow 70–75 feet clearance for ships to pass underneath. The new railway viaducts and track deviations were subject to inspection by officers of the Board of Trade. The Latchford viaduct, carrying the LNWR line between Warrington and Stockport, was completed before the end of 1892 and is seen here about to be tested by the weight of several locomotives. Goods trains only were allowed to use the viaducts for six months, after which they were declared safe for use by passenger trains. In the meantime, original lines had to remain intact, thereby preventing complete excavation of the canal channel. In this picture, it may be noted that the earth in the foreground has not yet been excavated, a length behind the photographer having had to remain undisturbed as support for the original railway track. Through the centre of the viaduct may be glimpsed a temporary timber bridge (not for trains) and, beyond, the stone piers of Latchford locks.

The Latchford viaduct was opened for goods traffic in February 1893, but not until July of that year did the Railway Inspectorate pass that and the viaduct at Acton Grange as fit for full use. The last pieces of land were thus released, and work could commence on cutting through the final sections.

After the opening of the western end of the canal as far as Ellesmere Port and the River Weaver, the next target was to complete the section which included Runcorn Docks. This was ready in mid-1893. Here, the old docks at Runcorn are filled with sailing ships. The lock in the foreground was the first of the flight of locks leading to the Bridgewater Canal. When the full length of the canal opened, sailing ships which could not lower their masts to pass under the fixed bridges, were able to transfer their cargoes to lighters at Runcorn.

At Barton, where the Bridgewater Canal crossed the Ship Canal, the original idea of providing a boat lift at each side, had been abandoned in favour of a swing aqueduct. To save time in emptying and re-filling, the aqueduct was designed as a sealed trough, to be swung whilst full of water. The shore ends of the canal were likewise sealed by watertight gates. The opening of the new aqueduct was delayed by a mishap on one of the approaches, for when the water was admitted in May 1893, part of the bed collapsed. The repair work was not completed until 21st August 1893, when the swing aqueduct was used for the first time. The demolition of Brindley's 1761 stone aqueduct then began. To carry out this work in the dry, the ends were sealed and a temporary coffer dam was erected in the centre of the waterway below. First, one side was blasted, and then the other. The new aqueduct is viewed here, from the Bridgewater Canal level, in process of swinging to permit the passage of a vessel on the Ship Canal beneath. It was not usual to swing the aqueduct complete with barge and towing horse. To economise on width, the tow path was carried across on a high platform inside the frame of the aqueduct.

The last dry cutting was finished on the 11th November 1893, and the filling of the Runcorn to Latchford section began. By the 25th November 1893 the Manchester Ship Canal was filled from end to end. Submerged dams and unfinished excavations were dredged away, and the Directors of the Company were able to make their first full passage of the canal on the 7th December 1893. The total expenditure had amounted to over £15½ millions. The opening took place on New Year's Day 1894, when Samuel Platt's steam yacht 'Norseman,' carrying the Company Directors, led a procession of 71 ships from Latchford to the terminal docks. The 'Pioneer,' a steamer owned by the Co-Operative Wholesale Society, unloaded a cargo of sugar on that first day. On the 21st May 1894 Queen Victoria (who had arrived in Manchester by train) boarded the yacht 'Enchantress' at Trafford Wharf, enjoyed a short sail as far as Mode Wheel Locks, and then formally declared the Manchester Ship Canal open. During her visit, the Queen conferred knighthoods on the Lord Mayor of Manchester and the Mayor of Salford. Edward Leader Williams and Bosdin Leech were similarly honoured some weeks later. The Queen's yacht is seen here after leaving Trafford Wharf.

The new docks attracted much attention in the early years. Passenger boats plied from the New Bailey landing stage, once the starting point for the old horse-drawn packet boats. Small steamers, such as the 'Pomona,' seen here in 1896, offered sightseeing tours round the docks, to Barton, or to points further along the Canal. The landing stage is now the site of the 'Mark Addy' public house, named after a heroic swimmer who rescued people from the river.

The 'Port of Manchester' is technically an elongated harbour, with dock facilities at intervals throughout its entire length of 36 miles. A Ship Canal Passenger Steamer Company was established, offering through sailings to Liverpool via the Ship Canal. The starting point was Trafford Wharf, where their paddle steamer 'United States' is seen moored. The passenger traffic flourished whilst the Canal was still a novelty, but afterwards failed.

The greatest attraction for visitors to the Canal was the Barton Swing Aqueduct, here seen with the swing road bridge beyond, both open to permit the passage of an outward-bound sailing vessel, towed by the ex-Bridgewater tug 'Dagmar.' Sailing vessels soon abandoned passage along the full length of the canal, their owners preferring to avoid towing charges.

Where the straightened course of the Ship Canal had cut across meanders of the Irwell, sections of the old river remained. One such length was at Irlam, by the Boat House Inn. This had once been a busy calling point for the packet-boats, where the innkeeper's duties had included the operation of the ferry to Flixton. After the opening of the Ship Canal, the inn became isolated on a quiet backwater.

# OPERATION 1894–1918

Plans for the terminal docks underwent several changes. The four small docks at Pomona (formerly the site of Pomona Gardens and zoo, and located mainly in Stretford — only part of No. 1 Dock was within the Manchester city boundary), were intended for coastwise shipping only. Opposite to them, in the Ordsall district of Salford, was to be Dock Number 5. Work on this was never completed, and it was later built over. It was decided that only one channel was necessary beneath Trafford Road, so the original course of the Irwell (on the left) was filled in with material dredged from the new cut, the fixed bridge remaining in place, and providing an underpass for railway lines. The nearer end of the channel remained as a useful mooring point for small vessels, barges and the fire boat. The main channel was crossed by the Trafford Road Swing Bridge. Docks 6–8, for ocean-going ships, were constructed on the western side of Trafford Road. Bottom left are Mode Wheel Locks, close to Manchester Racecourse (which also was in Salford), later to be the site of the large Number 9 Dock. Bottom right is part of the area bought in 1896 to be developed as the Trafford Park Industrial Estate. The tower of the No.1 Grain Elevator on Trafford Wharf may be noted on the opposite bank from the Racecourse.

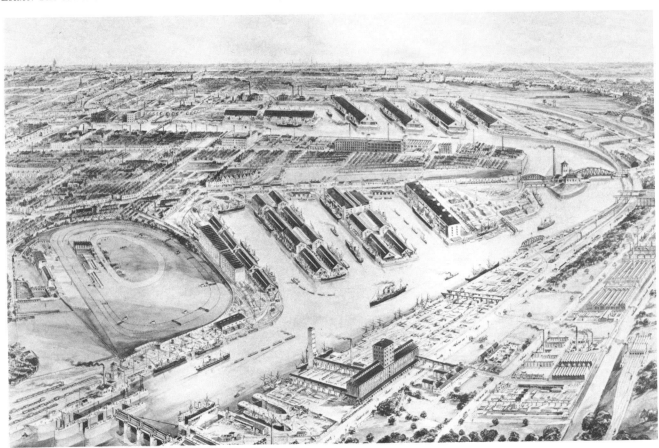

Of the seven swing road bridges along the length of the Canal, that at Trafford Road, Salford, was the furthest inland. It was the busiest in terms of road traffic, but least busy in terms of shipping movements. Only the smaller coastal steamers bound for Pomona Docks passed through, but it still swung often enough to cause delay and frustration for workers in Trafford Park, where the reason for late arrival was often due to being 'bridged.' Weighing 1800 tons, it was the heaviest swing bridge in the country, and was first successfully turned in December 1892. The machinery was operated by hydraulic power, and the pump house and the chimney of the boiler house are on the left, the operator's cabin being hidden from view. Beyond, in Trafford Road, may be seen the fixed bridge spanning the original course of the Irwell.

Westward from the Salford side of Trafford Bridge was the truncated portion of the original river course, used as a mooring for barges. On the left is the 'Firefly,' a twin-screw, twin-boilered vessel fitted out by Merryweather of London as a fire-fighting boat. The 'Firefly' had pumps capable of throwing 4000 gallons of water per minute. One boiler was kept permanently in steam so that the boat could be moved promptly in an emergency to any part of the docks. The crew had to fire the second boiler to help power the pumps. The 'Gamewell Fire Alarm System' was installed around the docks. Glass-fronted boxes, each with its own key and number, were sited around the 6½ miles of quays. By breaking the glass and turning the key, the alarm was raised and, at the same time, the location was automatically indicated to the boat crew and to the Manchester and Salford Fire Brigades. Whilst the 'Firefly' was moving to the required point, firemen from the towns' brigades would be on their way to assist the Ship Canal team. Spanning the canal is the railway swing bridge, built in 1895 to connect the Trafford Wharf lines (on the left) with those on the Salford side.

The Manchester Ship Canal Company maintained its own Dock Police Force and Fire Brigade, formed on the 26th December 1893, a few days before the opening of the full length of the Canal. Constables were sworn in by magistrates under Acts of 1840 and 1847, and their jurisdiction extended over the length of the Canal, and included the Bridgewater Canal and all Ship Canal premises. Duties included security checks, searches, co-operation with H.M.Customs, prevention of theft, and the general maintenance of law and order on Ship Canal land. The force rose in number from 16 in 1894 to a peak of over a hundred after World War II. Members wore uniforms similar to those of the Manchester City Police, except for the Company badge on the helmet. In the early days all members had to have fire-fighting training, and a hand-drawn fire-cart (here with a member in fireman's uniform) was equipped by the Salford firm of John Morris & Company. A 'Gamewell' system similar to the

fire alarm installation was used by the police at night to record progress on patrol. Failure to register the passing of a box by a given time meant that something was amiss, or that the officer had gone missing. One of the oldest private police forces in the country, after 99 years its remaining 25 officers were replaced by guards from a security company at the end of January 1993.

Dock workers queue for their pay at the Salford office in July 1897. The board above the hatch is advertising services at the Salford Dock Mission. The contractor's steam locomotive 'Weaver,' which remained on dock duties until sold to another contractor in 1898, is in the background.

It was important to establish facilities for the repair of ships. The dry docks opened in February 1894, followed by the floating, or pontoon dock in September. This "ugly monster," huge and unwieldy, together with an earlier one for Ellesmere Port, had been "provided by Newcastle gentlemen" and towed safely from the Tyne for a thousand miles around the coast and up the Canal. It was moored close to the entrance to the dry docks, just above Mode Wheel Locks, and is seen here accommodating a Greek ship.

As well as the general warehousing facilities provided on the docks, specialist installations included a Grain Elevator on Trafford Wharf, where the pneumatic apparatus was capable of sucking 350 tons per hour from a ship and distributing it into any one of 268 storage bins. Operations included weighing, sacking, and discharging into up to 40 railway wagons, barges, or carts simultaneously.

From the Grain Elevator main building could be seen the rear of its tower and the expanse of the Manchester Racecourse, later to be the site of No.9 Dock. The vessels moored on the Racecourse side of the canal are unloading timber, on what was then a rather cramped area. One of the small tugs is towing two barges loaded with skips from the dredgers.

Transit sheds were erected between wharves, some with under-cover facilities for transferring goods into railway wagons or carts. The interior of the shed on No.7 Dock shows mixed cargo storage on three levels, with railway tracks alongside.

Despite the optimism surrounding its opening, and the fact that ships' dues to Manchester were not charged for seven years, the Ship Canal was not an immediate success. Many ship-owners continued to use established ports, and some formed an alliance, with the aim of keeping up rates and restricting traffic to Liverpool or Glasgow. Others believed that large ships could not navigate the Canal safely. However, Christopher Furness, of Furness Withy & Company, and other shippers in the north-east, helped to secure a two-year contract for the Indian cotton trade, for at that time the import of raw cotton and the export of finished cotton textiles was believed to be the main basis for traffic on the canal. Furness was also interested in developing the North American trade, as

a result of which the Manchester Liners Company was formed in 1898 with two medium-sized second-hand ships. The first vessel built especially for Manchester Liners was the 'Manchester City' of 1899, a large and fast refrigerator ship, with telescopic masts to enable her to pass beneath the bridges. Her success in negotiating the waterway to Manchester did much to boost confidence in the safety of the Canal. She is seen approaching the Manchester Corporation Foreign Animals Wharf, just below Mode Wheel Locks. Tug 'Mercia' is alongside.

In the first six months of operation, 630 sea-going vessels docked at Manchester, but it took over three years for traffic to build up to a reasonable level. A factor in the success of the Ship Canal was the development of Trafford Park as an industrial estate. Marshall Stevens, the Canal Company's first General Manager before moving in 1896 to become the Managing Director in Trafford Park, attracted factory owners to the Park with the prospect of easy and cheap access to deep water transport. A railway network was set up within the Park to serve the various sites, and in 1898 connections were made to the dock railway system. As the docks became busier, the Canal Company expanded its own railway network and made connections to the main lines. Ship Canal locomotives had running rights over the Trafford Park lines, though until 1922 the Trafford Park Estates Company maintained a small locomotive fleet of its own. The Canal Company's

railway swing bridge is seen here from the Trafford Park side, with the Trafford Wharf coaling stage in the foreground. A train is crossing from the Salford side, where the sidings behind No.6 Dock were the only ones available in the early days.

The Ship Canal system eventually expanded to become the largest privately-owned railway in Britain, with 75 locomotives, 2,700 wagons, and over 200 miles of track on the dock estates and alongside the canal. At the outset, some of the locomotives engaged

on the construction contract were retained for use by the Company, others were purchased new after 1897. The locomotives were named, some after places along the canal, others after major ports or countries of the world. Not until 1914–15 were numbers allocated to the engines. 'Valencia' was supplied new in 1902, later becoming number 25 in the fleet. The practice of naming the engines ceased during the 1914–18 War, and nameplates were removed. It is alleged that the driver of the locomotive 'Hamburg' was the target of threats at this time, but the substitution of numbers for names was probably a matter of clerical convenience.

At Partington a coaling basin was established to re-fuel the ships. It had seven tips operated by hydraulic machinery. The coaster 'Mabel' is about to receive a cargo of coal by chute from the loaded wagon on the hoist. After tipping, the platform lifted the empty wagon to join others on the return line, then collected the next full one. Empty wagons rolled back to the sidings by gravity. On the other side of the canal is the 'Iron Prince,' a Prince Line vessel, whose owner, John Knott, was an early supporter of the Ship Canal. His 'Belgian Prince' was one of the first ships to travel the whole length of the canal on the opening day.

On the north side of the canal, near Weaste, Andrew Knowles & Sons Limited, of Clifton Colliery, installed a steam crane of 25 tons capacity, which could lift a loaded railway wagon and tip its contents direct into the vessel alongside. This operation was much more labour-intensive than the Partington tips.

In the early years, the Ship Canal Company, lacking a sufficient number of tug-boats of its own, chartered Liverpool tugs to pilot vessels along the canal. In the western reaches of the canal, the Liverpool paddle-tug 'Merry Andrew' is stationed at the stern of a steamship, whilst a tug from the Alexandra Towing Company, also of Liverpool, leads the way.

The narrowness of the canal at certain points, the sharp turns, and the several locks, presented problems for the tugboat skippers. Screw tugs were efficient ahead of the tow, but when placed at the stern they were not so satisfactory. The old paddle-tugs acquired from the Bridgewater Company had the disadvantage that their engines could not drive the paddle wheels independently. On the River Tyne, paddle tugs with independent engines had been operating successfully, and the Company decided to assess their suitability on the canal. Two Tyne paddle tugs, the 'Ulysses' and the 'Hercules,' were chartered for a time to assist with traffic duties. A rare picture of the 'Hercules' at the stern of a steamship passing the Barton bridges confirms this trial, probably in 1902, after which the Company placed orders with South Shields builders for six paddle tugs in the period 1903–1907. These tugs had independent engines, and were specifically for stern-towing duties. Each one of them gave over 40 years service on the canal.

Although the canal proved a financial disappointment to its promoters in the first few years, it soon began to deal with a wide variety of imports and exports, and its docks became crowded with ships of all nations. By 1904, assessed by the value of goods handled, Manchester was rated as the fifth port of the United Kingdon, exceeded only by London, Liverpool, Hull and Glasgow. No.6 Dock, the smallest of those designed for ocean-going ships, is seen here with vessels moored two abreast.

The purchase of the Racecourse site, where the last race meeting took place at Easter 1901, gave possibilities for expansion, and enabled Manchester to rise to the position of fourth port of the United Kingdon. The huge No.9 Dock, over half-a-mile long, was planned, together with a railway marshalling yard. Traffic on the canal continued uninterrupted whilst excavations were made for the new dock. The quaysides and warehouses were built on piers, invisible once the dock was flooded, but seen here under construction. Wagons of the contractor Henry Lovatt, of Wolverhampton, stand on the temporary railway laid for the removal of spoil.

A dam separated the No.9 Dock excavation from the canal proper. It is here used as a temporary berth for the first 'Manchester Shipper,' a Manchester Liners vessel built in 1900. (Two later ships carried the same name.) When preparations were complete, a small breach was made in the top of the dam wall, allowing water from the main canal to spill over and gradually flood the new dock.

When the water level equalised, explosive charges were placed in holes drilled in the retaining wall, then detonated, causing it to collapse to the canal bed, after which a dredger and a steam ram cleared or hammered the remains to achieve the required depth. The dredger 'Mersey' waits on the left, whilst one of the charges breaks the wall.

No.9 Dock was opened on the 13th July 1905 by King Edward VII and Queen Alexandra. Two Mersey ferry boats, the 'Claughton' and the 'Bidston,' were chartered to carry guests ceremonially past the royal pavilion, which had been erected temporarily on the side of the new dock. The demolition of one of the old racecourse grandstands was deferred until after the royal visit, and was used for some of the thousands of onlookers who thronged to see the royal visitors. Today, the scene is vastly changed, but the spire of Stowell Memorial Church remains as a local landmark.

The new No.9 Dock shortly after the opening in 1905, has a steam ram at work in the foreground, whilst one of the paddle tugs sails from the dock to join the main canal. The vessel moored on the right is the 'Manchester Merchant' (built 1904 to replace an earlier 'Manchester Merchant' lost in 1903). Though the royal pavilion has gone, the grandstand remains. Warehouses on the left of the dock, and the Number 2 Grain Elevator, which stood at its head, were not built until much later.

Another vessel of Manchester Liners, the 'Manchester Corporation,' built 1899, seen from a warehouse roof in No.9 Dock. The open space on the left was developed into a timber storage area. Note the railway tracks and the row of cranes sited between ship and warehouse, enabling cargoes to be discharged direct into railway wagons if desired. The increasing traffic on the Ship Canal helped to bring prosperity to the region, and encouraged the management to consider deepening the channel from 26 to 28 feet so as to admit ships of greater draught. This was done in 1909 by raising the water level by two feet, rather than dredging to a greater depth.

The depth of the Suez Canal was 26 feet, so it was known that ships using that route from India, Australia and the Far East could also sail to Manchester. Consequently, imported goods increased in variety, and it was usual for imported tonnage to exceed that of the exports. Nevertheless, British manufactures were drawn from a surprisingly wide area for export via the Ship Canal to all parts of the world. Products from the Trafford Park factories and the immediate district were joined by others from further afield. The Prince Line offered regular services from Manchester to all Mediterranean ports, and here the 'Scottish Prince' of 1910 loads traction engines and agricultural machinery from Lincolnshire for delivery to Casablanca and Tunis. The 'Scottish Prince' had an interesting subsequent history. In 1917 during World War I, she was torpedoed, but did not sink, being repaired to remain in service until sold to Greek owners in 1937. Re-named 'Athinai,' she was sunk off Sicily during World War II in 1940.

Number 9 Dock in its heyday, seen from the eastern end, with the timber storage ground to the right. It was not uncommon for ships to moor two abreast whilst waiting for a vacant berth. Further expansion was envisaged, and there were plans for a No.10 Dock to run parallel with No.9, but these were never implemented. The outbreak of war in 1914 halted progress, and work on the No.2 Grain Elevator and additional warehouses was deferred.

In August 1918 the Ellerman liner 'City Of Exeter' brought American troops to Salford Docks. The ship (right) sported bizarre wartime camouflage paint. Along with her sister ships, 'City of Calcutta' and 'City Of Marseilles,' she made a number of voyages, each bringing some 116 officers and 1338 men along the canal en route for inland camps.

# THE INTER-WAR YEARS, 1919–1938

An unusual visitor to Manchester Docks was this captured German submarine, the U-111, placed on show in Pomona Docks in 1919.

A commercial postcard, produced by Sankey's of Barrow about 1922, shows the head of No.9 Dock and the new No.2 Grain Elevator. Additional warehouses were soon to occupy part of the wharf on the left. Imports for onward carriage to final destinations could be transferred direct to rail or road vehicles, or stored until collected. Some goods were transhipped for distribution via the network of smaller canals, being unloaded over the side of large steamers into barges. Here, smaller vessels have taken on cargoes of newsprint or grain. One of the small steam tugs ordered for the Bridgewater Canal system in the 1870s is towing a barge across the dock.

A later 1920s view of the main terminal docks includes the new warehouses and No.2 Grain Elevator on No.9 Dock (left) and the railway marshalling yard (centre). In the left foreground a ship of the Prince Line (identifiable by the Prince of Wales feathers on the funnel) is moored at Trafford Wharf, whilst opposite, having discharged her cargo, is the Manchester Liners vessel 'Manchester Importer.' She had been built in 1899 and was sold to Greek owners in 1927.

BIRDS EYE VIEW OF MANCHESTER DOCKS

At the end of No.8 Dock an extensive water basin allowed large vessels to be turned before commencing their outward voyage along the canal. At the opening it was claimed that a ship as large as the 'Great Eastern' could be turned easily. The tugs are in process of swinging an oil tanker. One of the most radical changes in imports was the carriage of oil in bulk, rather than in casks or drums. The first oil storage tanks had been installed at Mode Wheel in 1896, and afterwards additional tanks were sited at Weaste and Eccles on the Salford bank, and at Barton on the Trafford Park side of the canal. These oil wharves were below Mode Wheel Locks, but, after discharging their oil, the larger tankers were obliged to proceed through the locks to the turning basin in order to gain sufficient room to swing.

The 'Manchester Regiment,' built 1922, was a turbine steamer. At 7930 tons gross and 11,572 deadweight, she was Manchester Liners' biggest ship in the period between the wars. Her record from the Mersey to Quebec was seven days and nine hours. She is seen here in No.9 Dock in 1934. She was lost on 4th December 1939, shortly after the outbreak of war. Whilst sailing without navigation lights, she was struck by the 'Oropesa,' which had been detached from a convoy for special duties.

The original headquarters of the Ship Canal Company were at 41 Spring Gardens, in Manchester city centre. In 1926 the new 'Ship Canal House' was opened in King Street. An attractive feature of the building was the statue of Neptune on the roof, though too high to be noticed by many who passed by in the street below. This building was vacated in 1982.

Similarly, the Dock Offices, which for 33 years had been a warren of rather primitive wooden huts on the Old Trafford side of Trafford Bridge, were replaced in 1927 by a new building in Trafford Road, Salford, close to the entrance gates by No.8 Dock.

No.8 Dock in the early 1930s has a collection of no fewer than ten tugs awaiting the call to duty. The Dock Office is seen in the middle distance.

The steamer 'Truthful,' a regular on the Manchester — London service, makes a splash as her engines go astern to slow the ship as she prepares to halt in Irlam Locks. Small to medium-sized vessels were allowed to proceed along the canal without tugs. Self-employed pilots were available to guide ships, but masters who regularly used the canal often held their own certificate of competence issued by the Company. To become a pilot, one had first to be a Merchant Navy officer for at least four years, probably holding a mate's certificate, be trained as a helmsman, and pass an examination as a second-class pilot. On board, the pilot had a special relationship with the master, and had to achieve a close liaison between ship's crew, the tugboat men, and the shore staff.

Inward bound at Irlam, the Hull steamer 'Kotka' and paddle tug 'Old Trafford' rise in the large lock, whilst an outward-bound vessel is lowered in the small lock alongside.

The 'Manchester Producer,' outward bound for Canadian ports, demonstrates the limited clearance for large vessels as she passes under Irlam viaduct. The topmost portions of the masts have been telescoped for the passage along the canal. This vessel had begun life as the Furness Withy liner 'Start Point' in 1916, but had been purchased by Manchester Liners in 1921. Sold prior to the outbreak of war in 1939 to the Board of Trade, she became the 'Botwey,' (the Board of Trade ships had the appropriate prefix 'Bot'), but was lost off north-west Scotland in 1941 when torpedoed by a German U-Boat.

The publisher of this commercial postcard of Latchford Locks entitled it 'A Busy Time.' The occasion appears to be a holiday, as visitors are being allowed to climb a ladder to board the steamer 'Wandsworth' in the foreground. An outward-bound ship occupies the main lock, whilst a paddle tug is lowered in the small chamber alongside. Behind the 'Wandsworth,' another vessel, assisted by tugs, waits to enter the large lock. Shore staff, controlling ship movements, arranged the meeting place of two large vessels with tugs, and in this case it would have been agreed for the tugs to hold the inward-bound vessel in the lower sluiceway to enable the other ship to clear the locks.

To enable people, animals, or vehicles to cross the canal where there was no bridge, ferries were provided by the Company at several points along the route. At certain locks, pedestrians had a right-of-way across the walkways atop the lock gates. The original cable-hauled ferry at Irlam bore the title 'M.S.C. No.1 Horse Ferry.' Brass checks, or tokens, for the ferry fare were sold in advance at eightpence per dozen. In later years a diesel-engined vessel was provided — at a higher fare !

At Bob's Lane Ferry, Cadishead, a rowing boat sufficed for many years to carry people across to Partington. A motor launch replaced the rowing boat, but by 1993 the average number of passengers carried per day had fallen to 69. The subsidy had been reduced, repairs costed at £31,000 were needed to the jetty, and the ferry service faced closure.

In 1929 a Royal Navy destroyer flotilla, consisting of five ships, the 'Campbell,' 'Wakeful,' 'Wessex,' 'Westcott,' and 'Wolfhound,' paid a week's courtesy visit to Manchester, and offered unusual sights as they passed along the canal. They arrived at Eastham Locks having sailed from Oban. Destroyer D47, H.M.S. 'Westcott' arrives at Trafford Wharf on the 18th June.

The destroyers proved a popular attraction. Crowds negotiated the railway tracks on Trafford Wharf to inspect the ships. During the visit one Able Seaman from the 'Wakeful' married a Manchester girl, his mess-deck colleagues hauling the bridal carriage. The crews were entertained by the city council, and enjoyed trips to Belle Vue and Blackpool. The local press reported that the captain of the 'Wolfhound' discovered his wireless operator running a boot and shoe repair shop from quarters on the ship, and found that he had taken in work not only for his own messmates, but also for crews of other vessels moored in the docks.

The end of No.9 Dock in 1930 shows the Prince Liner 'Syrian Prince,' riding high in the water, moored by the timber storage area. 'Soldier Prince' and 'Cyprian Prince' are moored alongside each other further down the dock. One of the floating grain elevators is at work alongside the 'Paris City' (registered at Bideford) on the right, whilst in the foreground one of the unlovely workhorses of the docks ferries workers across the canal.

An aerial photograph of July 1932 includes the Manchester Dry Docks. The floating pontoon is empty, but the three dry docks are fully occupied with large steamers. The largest dry dock was 535 feet long, and the width of all three was 65 feet, the same width as the locks on the upper reaches of the canal. Mode Wheel Locks provide a mooring point for one of the floating cranes, and the oil storage tanks may be seen top left. Bottom right a steamer and barges are moored by the British Oil and Cake Mills, which produced cattle feed.

In 1926–28 the Newcastle firm of Armstrong Whitworth constructed five ships specially adapted for the carriage of railway rolling stock and other heavy items. The ships had been commissioned by Christen Smith, of Oslo. The 'Belpamela' is seen in 1938 starting for Buenos Aires after loading subway coaches at Ellesmere Port. The 'Belpamela' was acquired as a prize by the German invaders of Norway in 1940, but was returned to her owners in 1945. Whilst on a voyage from New York to Cherbourg in 1947, some of her cargo broke loose during an Atlantic storm, causing such profound damage that the ship was lost.

There were a number of locomotive builders in the Manchester area and it was not unusual to see railway engines from Beyer Peacock, Nasmyth Wilson, or the Vulcan Foundry lined up for export via Salford Docks. A sister ship to the 'Belpamela' is seen at Salford Quay opposite to the Dry Docks, where temporary railway track has been laid to accommodate Nasmyth locomotives awaiting shipment in 1927 for South Indian Railways. Far right are Vulcan engines for the Bengal Railway.

More rolling stock for export. Coaches for Palestine Railways are hauled across the sidings behind No.9 Dock by M.S.C. locomotive number 39 'Sydney.' The year is about 1935, and the engine's name is painted on the box above the leading wheel. At this date the locomotives were carefully painted and neatly lined-out. The original locomotive livery was green, later changed to slate grey, often mistaken for black due to the liberal coatings of oil.

The increasing amount of crude oil imported via the canal led the Company to consider the establishment of additional oil docks. Safety considerations made the choice of an isolated location desirable, the marshes around Stanlow being seen as an ideal site. A specialist oil dock was constructed on the estuary side of the canal at Stanlow and opened in 1922. It was suitably distanced from the refineries on the marsh, the oil being pumped to the storage tanks via pipes laid beneath the canal. Soon, the export of petroleum products became an important trade, and a second, and larger, oil dock was sited alongside the first. The official opening of Stanlow No.2 Dock took place on the 26th May 1933, when the British Petroleum tanker 'British Duchess' entered. The tender 'Ryde' of Liverpool was in attendance (right) carrying invited guests.

An aerial view of Nos. 6, 7. and 8 Docks in 1933 was taken during the period of the trade depression, when several Manchester Liners vessels were laid up for lack of cargoes. Two are moored abreast in No.6 Dock (right) and another at the head of No.7 Dock (centre). The rows of terraced houses in the Ordsall district, and the mills and factories of Manchester beyond, form a backdrop to the scene.

In July 1935 the old 'Firefly' fire tender was replaced by a new dual-purpose vessel, built by Henry Robb at Leith, and, as with the first 'Firefly,' fitted with fire-fighting equipment by the Merryweather Company. The new 'Firefly' was a fire and salvage tug, but was also intended for general use about the docks. It proved its worth during the air raids of the Second World War, when the enemy tried to destroy or halt shipping on the canal. The second 'Firefly' was a powerful tug, and although intended to be based above Mode Wheel Locks in case of urgent need in the terminal docks, it engaged in general towing duties along the length of the canal. It remained in service for 30 years, being sold to breakers in 1965.

Floating pneumatic grain elevators are overshadowed by the giant No.2 Elevator at the head of No.9 Dock in 1936. The main elevator had a storage capacity of 40,000 tons, and was connected to the discharging berths by conveyor belts in subways running under the wharves. The floating elevator unloading the Greek ship on the left is discharging grain directly into a barge moored on its other side. On the right is the Ropner Shipping Company's 'Hindpool,' built 1928, and registered in West Hartlepool. The Ropner Company suffered badly in World War 2, losing no fewer than 33 ships due to enemy action. The 'Hindpool' was one such loss, being torpedoed and sunk off West Africa by the U 124.

Timber continued to be a major import at several points along the canal. The steamer 'Harald' discharges cut planks direct into railway wagons on Trafford Wharf in 1935.

At the Ellesmere Port timber wharf, the steamship 'Carl Cords' unloads logs. The cranes worked from broad gauge track, leaving room between their supports for standard gauge railway wagons to move freely.

The timber ships often carried deck cargo, which looked more alarming than it really was. The steamship 'Atlantic' arrived from Archangel on the 17th June 1935 with a cargo of 1364 cubic fathoms of pit props, of which 445 cublic fathoms were carried on deck, supported at the sides by logs lashed in an upright position. One wonders how the crewmen managed to move about the deck.

At Runcorn, the old docks which once opened direct on to the estuary, were operated by the Company's Bridgewater Department, and remained in use for smaller vessels. Ships over 350 feet long, or with a beam of over 50 feet, or drawing more than 17½ feet of water, could not be accommodated. The Hughes Holden ship 'Moelfre Rose' in the Alfred Dock unloads a cargo of china clay from Cornwall.

Vessels of the Prince Line offered a service from Manchester to any Mediterranean ports as inducement offered, bringing back mixed cargoes of Middle-Eastern produce. The 'Lancastrian Prince' was a regular visitor between 1921 and 1938. She is seen passing Barton, bringing in a load of Egyptian cotton from Alexandria. The 'Lancastrian Prince' was sold to French owners in 1938. Renamed the 'Champenois,' she became yet another wartime casualty, being sunk off Casablanca in 1941.

The 'Pacific' liners of the Furness Withy group offered a fortnightly service from Manchester via the Panama Canal to the west coast ports of North America. The 'Pacific President,' one of four similar ships built in 1928, is seen entering Mode Wheel Locks in July 1936, outward bound with general cargo for Vancouver. At the stern is the 1905 paddle tug 'Eccles.' The 'Pacific President' was another wartime loss. She was torpedoed on a voyage from the United Kingdom to New York in December 1940.

With the revival of trade in the late 1930s, Manchester Liners took delivery of three new ships between 1935 and 1938. The 'Manchester City,' the second ship to bear that name, was photographed arriving at Eastham on delivery from the builders in August 1937. At the outbreak of war, the Manchester Liners fleet consisted of ten vessels, of which three were lost, and the 'Manchester City' was requisitioned by the Admiralty. She first became an auxiliary 'mother' ship to minelayers, and afterwards was stationed in the Indian Ocean, playing a full part in the Far Eastern war. She survived to return to her rightful owners in post-war years, and remained in service until 1964.

# WORLD WAR II, 1939–1945

The work of the Ship Canal assumed national importance in the period of World War II. The waterway was kept open, in spite of frequent and heavy air raids in 1940–41, during which the docks and the factories of Trafford Park became particular targets. In the 1940s, some 75,000 workers were employed in Trafford Park, many engaged in the manufacture of munitions, tanks, aircraft, and other essential war supplies. The Dry Docks undertook repair work of a sort not known before, when vessels damaged by torpedoes or gunfire limped up the canal to Trafford Wharf. Merchant ships crossed the Atlantic in large convoys, so that Royal Navy escorts could offer some protection from marauding U-Boats. For camouflage, merchant ships were repainted in a drab livery of battleship grey, and means of identification, such as names and funnel markings, were removed. A freighter fitted with gun turrets fore and aft, and with life rafts ready for immediate use, is here assisted into No.9 Dock by the paddle tug 'Irlam.'

A wartime view along No.9 Dock from the roof of the No.2 Grain elevator. The gun turrets had been fitted hastily to most ocean-going vessels as defence against surface attack by enemy warships or aircraft. The No.1 Grain Elevator, formerly a landmark on Trafford Wharf (top left), had been destroyed by incendiary bombs during an air raid in 1940.

In addition to the fixed wharfside facilities, the Ship Canal Company had to provide specialist equipment capable of being moved around as required. The floating cranes were able to hoist and carry large or heavy items for loading over the off-side of ships at the quays. The largest floating crane was able to deal with weights up to 250 tons, and had a lift of 21 feet. It is seen here near the end of No.9 Dock in 1944, shepherded by paddle tug 'Barton' and another, whilst hoisting a sheeted railway wagon.

# POST-WAR RECOVERY AND BOOM 1946–1959

After the 1939–45 War, the docks slowly returned to peacetime activities. This 1947 aerial photograph, looking across the main terminal docks towards Weaste, shows most vessels restored to their pre-war livery. Two Manchester Liners are berthed in their usual place in No.9 Dock, whilst a third is moored in No.7. Bottom left is the Trafford Road swing bridge, and above it the railway swing bridge. The original 1895 railway bridge, which carried only a single line, was found to be too restrictive for the free flow of wartime traffic, and a replacement bridge with double track was completed in 1943. The old bridge was left for a time permanently in the open position, and may be seen alongside Trafford Wharf (left), just above the newer bridge. Mode Wheel Locks appear top left.

In the post-war years, restrictions remained in force until the tonnage of shipping lost was replaced, and industry reverted to peacetime activities. Stanlow developed into a major oil centre, second only to London, with pipe-lines for the distribution of refined products. Two ocean-going tankers are seen in 1947 discharging crude oil in the large No.2 Dock, and two coastal tankers are moored in the smaller dock. Another large tanker is berthed in the lay-bye on the left, whilst tugs guide a freighter along the canal in the direction of Eastham. The mudflats of the Mersey estuary appear top right.

The Lancashire Steel Corporation works at Irlam likewise returned to peacetime production. The steamer 'Pencarrow' is discharging ore at the wharf in 1949. (Thirty years later, in 1979, the steelworks closed.) The 'Anglia,' a Swedish Lloyd ship, built in 1946, having just left Irlam Locks, passes unassisted down the canal. The Swedish Lloyd Company offered services from Gothenburg to Manchester via the north of Scotland route.

Trade revived and the canal was busy in the 1950s. The 60-ton self-propelled floating crane loads a 75 m.p.h. diesel electric locomotive, built in 1952 by the English Electric Company for the Egyptian State Railways. The vessel, appropriately, is the Prince Line's 'Egyptian Prince,' the fifth vessel to carry this name, built in 1951. Two crew members are employed on what were regular tasks when in port, cleaning and painting.

The chief item of maintenance expenditure on the canal was the never-ending task of dredging. To ensure an adequate depth of water for the deep-draughted vessels using the port, dredging was necessary in the three-mile channel approaching Eastham Locks, as well as along the whole 36 miles of the canal. Using electronic equipment for hydrographic surveys, it was possible to plan a programme of dredging priority with up-to-the-minute information about the depth of water in the docks and along the canal. The silt was lifted from the bottom of the canal by bucket, grab, or suction, and the material was usually loaded into skips for disposal elsewhere. The 'Irwell,' a bucket-dredger, is here at work near Pomona Docks. Closely allied to the dredging activities, were the responsibilities of lock staff in setting and operating the sluices to maintain the correct water level.

A 30-ton 'de-masting' crane was maintained at Eastham for the purpose of removing and replacing topmasts and funnels so that large ships could safely pass beneath the fixed bridges. The Strick liner 'Serbistan' (built 1944, and bearing a name which was used more than once) is moored by the crane on the south bank. Note the funnel tops on the bank alongside, awaiting their owners' return from Manchester. A dredger is moored by the embankment separating the canal from the Mersey estuary.

In 1939 Furness Withy had eight ships on the services to west coast ports of North America, only three of which survived the war, and one of those the 'Pacific Enterprise,' was wrecked in 1949. However, in 1947 as trade revived, one 'victory' ship and four 'liberty' ships, built hastily in wartime to a standard pattern, were acquired to replace lost tonnage. The 'Pacific Importer' (ex-'John Tipton') was one of the 'liberty' ships, and is seen here passing Barton on her way to Manchester in 1950. The stern tug is the paddler 'Rixton,' built in 1905 and withdrawn after 50 years' service in 1955. Furness Withy's 'liberty ships' were sold on for service elsewhere as new replacements became available in 1952–54.

The 'Pacific Exporter' was one of four sister vessels built in 1928. At the Furness Withy berth at the head of No.8 Dock, she is seen on what must have been one of her last visits to Manchester, for she was sold in 1951. She is taking on an export cargo of British motor vehicles for Canada and the United States. The floating crane is silhouetted against the night sky.

The 'Pacific Fortune,' new in 1948 from Blythswood, Scotstoun, forms the backdrop for a study of one of the Bridgewater Department's fleet of lorries, a reminder of the Ship Canal Company's involvement in the distribution of goods by road. The lorry is carrying rolls of newsprint. It is a curious fact that, starting with the 'Pacific Fortune', the names chosen for the new Furness Withy 'Pacific' ships in the 1948–58 period began to spell the word FURNESS with the first letter of the second name. Thus, after the 'Pacific Fortune,' came the 'Pacific Unity' followed by 'Reliance,' 'Northwest,' 'Envoy,' and 'Stronghold.' The sequence was never quite completed, however, for the 'Pacific Stronghold' of 1958 was the last new ship, and two subsequent vessels were temporary and short-lived transfers in 1970, in which year the service ceased, and the ships were sold.

The 'Pacific Unity' was built in 1948 by Laing of Sunderland. Her beam measured 63 feet 5 inches (the 'Pacific Fortune' was 63'6"), and for a time these ships held the record as being the widest vessels to negotiate the 65-feet-wide locks of the Ship Canal. (Only the Eastham entrance lock was wider, at 80 feet.) However, in 1954 they were surpassed by the Ropner Line's 'Swiftpool,' measuring 63'7", and in 1966 by the Strick Line's new 'Serbistan,' which sailed to Manchester on three occasions, and which, with a 63'10" beam, must remain the widest vessel ever to navigate the upper portion of the canal. The 'Pacific Unity' is seen here on her maiden voyage in Barton Locks, illustrating the tight clearance of the lock sides with only inches to spare. The tug is the 'Arrow.'

The 'Manchester Division,' built in 1918, survived the war years, during which she saw service in the Red Sea and Indian Ocean. With the delivery of new vessels in the early 1950s, she was withdrawn and sold for scrap in 1953, having sailed for Manchester Liners for 35 years. She is seen here leaving Eastham Locks outward bound for Montreal in 1951. It was the custom for the city of Montreal to award a gold-headed cane to the captain of the first ship to navigate through the breaking ice and reach the port each Spring, and Manchester Liners captains were frequent recipients of this accolade.

The 'Manchester Progress,' built 1938, was also involved in war work, being one of the last vessels to leave Rangoon in 1941, afterwards ferrying supplies to forces in the Middle East. Returning to the Atlantic run, she remained in service until 1966. The 1907 paddle tug 'Old Trafford' controls her stern as the vessel enters Barton Locks on her way to Manchester. Designed specifically to operate as stern tugs, the broad beam and shallow draught of the six paddle tugs, together with their manoeuvrability, made them superior to screw tugs for the awkward task of stern towing in the restricted waters of the canal. The 'Old Trafford,' lying astern with crossed ropes, is here inching the bigger ship's stern slightly to starboard as she positions her correctly between the lock walls. The 'Old Trafford' was sold in 1950 for further service on the Tyne, where she was renamed 'Reliant.' Withdrawn from service at Seaham in 1969, she was acquired by the National Maritime Museum at Greenwich, where she now rests (as the 'Reliant') in the New Neptune Hall.

Manchester Liners embarked upon a rebuilding programme to replace the five ships lost during the war. A new 'Manchester Regiment' arrived in 1947, 'Manchester Merchant' in 1951, and an order for a new 'Manchester Spinner' was placed with Cammell Lairds. At the same time, the Company decided to offer direct services to ports on the Great Lakes, and two specially-designed small ships were ordered. On the 30th January 1952 a dual launching ceremony took place at Birkenhead. First, the large 'Manchester Spinner' slid into the water, to be followed a few minutes later by the 'Manchester Pioneer.' A few weeks later, this small ship was joined in the fitting-out basin by her sister ship, the 'Manchester Explorer.'

The 'Manchester Pioneer' was completed by April 1952 and started the first all-British service to the Great Lakes. On her first voyage she carried a gift from the Manchester Chamber of Commerce to the Toronto Board of Trade, namely a ship's bell, which is sounded to call members to order. Also on board was the first 'electronic brain' produced by Ferranti for the University of Toronto. 'Manchester Explorer,' was ready in the following month. The two vessels, drawing only 14 feet of water, had to pass through no fewer than 21 locks inwards, some of which were only six inches wider than the ships. They were able to navigate small creeks and rivers with such success that an additional small vessel, the 'Vigor,' was purchased from Norwegian owners and renamed the 'Manchester Prospector' before joining the Lakes service in 1953. The 'Manchester Explorer' extended the service as far as Chicago in 1955, and in 1959, when the St.Lawrence Seaway opened, Manchester Liners sailed to Duluth, at the head of Lake Superior, to bring out cargoes of grain and edible oils. The opening of the Seaway rendered the small 'lakers' largely redundant, but in 1960 the 'Manchester Pioneer' was lengthened by 40 feet in Manchester Dry Docks and served for another three years.

The Ship Canal earned the nickname of 'The Big Ditch.' An aerial view of the waterway near Latchford illustrates the reason. The Knutsford Road swing bridge is open in the foreground to admit the passage of a large outward bound oil tanker. The railway viaduct and Latchford locks lie beyond.

An Esso Company oil tanker, the 'Esso Plymouth,' is towed along the canal near Warrington by the tug 'Bison.' Large vessels such as this could be swung only in the basins at Stanlow or Manchester.

The import of crude oil increased to such an extent, and the bulk carriers grew so large, that the Ship Canal Company constructed a new four-berth dock, with a separate entrance lock, at Eastham. Storage tanks were concealed below ground, and pipeline connections were laid to the refineries at Stanlow. The new dock was 40 feet deep, with an entrance lock 807 by 100 feet, capable of admitting vessels which were too large to sail in the canal. Named the Queen Elizabeth II Dock, it was opened officially in January 1954, and offered facilities for the loading and discharge of petroleum products, chemicals, and edible oils in bulk. Three large tankers are seen in the new dock, whilst a smaller tanker is about to leave the main canal via the exit lock. With the development of giant 'supertankers,' even the new dock proved too restrictive, and the larger vessels began to dock in more open water at the Tranmere Oil Terminal, their oil being piped to Stanlow.

Liquid of a different kind came along the canal in the 1950s. 'The Lady Grania' and 'The Lady Gwendolen,' vessels belonging to Arthur Guinness of Dublin, crossed the Irish Sea to make regular visits to Pomona Docks, Manchester. 'The Lady Grania,' new in 1952, was photographed near Barton in 1954, returning empty to Dublin. At this period, she sailed along the canal weekly.

The Guinness ships carried some liquid in barrels, the rest in transportable stainless steel containers, which were conveyed from the ship to bottling plants. Containers are being lifted from the ship's hold at Pomona Docks in 1954. In the early 1970s the Guinness boats ceased to come to Manchester, the base being moved to Runcorn, where administration, importation, and distribution were combined in one depot.

The main terminal docks, with their bevy of large, modern, smartly-painted ships, possessed a certain air of romance, redolent of far-off places. By contrast, the smaller Pomona Docks lacked glamour, and latterly acquired a definite down-market flavour. Here were to be found the tramps of the coastal trade, often dirty ancient coal-burners, with grimy and chipped paintwork, offering a generally neglected appearance. The dockside equipment seemed to match, with elderly steam cranes supplementing the ships' gear. Dock No.1, by Cornbrook Road, became the regular discharging point for Cooper's River Sand boats. William Cooper often purchased old coasters to bring sand and gravel along the canal to Pomona. He named the vessels after members of his family. Two of his ships are seen here, that on the right being the 'Mary P. Cooper,' later to be a source of embarrassment to the Ship Canal Company when she sank near Stockton Heath in 1961.

As a wartime evacuee, the writer became fascinated by the ageing steam coasters operated by Robert Gardner of Lancaster. These small vessels carried bulk cargoes of coal, limestone, gravel, sand, even flour and Indian corn, between west coast ports wherever inducement offered. The 'Multistone,' new to United Stone Firms of Bristol in 1910, passed to a Newcastle firm before being acquired by Gardner in 1934. In 1940, she was requisitioned by the Ministry of War Transport, and disappeared northwards to act as a supply tender for warships on the Clyde. In August 1954, the author, armed with a Ship Canal permit for photography, was delighted to find her in No.4 Dock at Pomona, discharging china clay from Cornwall. She was Gardner's last steamship, and was sold the following year. Crew members would gain no sleep if the ship negotiated the canal during the hours of darkness, and would be kept awake during the day when unloading was being done by a noisy steam crane with a grab. By evening, the ship would be ready to return down the canal, the crew steam-cleaning the hold on the way, ready to receive a new cargo the following morning.

Ships of the Belfast Steamship Company, a member of the Coast Lines group, were regular visitors to Pomona Docks. In the early 1950s the Company operated eight vessels, built at various dates between 1922 and 1938. They carried general cargo between Northern Ireland, Liverpool and Manchester. The Company's naming policy ensured that all their vessels began with the word 'Ulster.' The oldest ship at the time was the 'Ulster Mariner,' (built 1922) seen discharging at Pomona in 1954. The steam crane is transferring crates from ship to warehouse.

Moored out of use in Pomona Docks in 1954 was the last surviving Ship Canal paddle tug, the 'Rixton,' built in 1905. Although not officially withdrawn until 1955, she had evidently been out of use for some time. The brass mounting in front of the wheelhouse had once housed the ship's bell. The other five paddlers had been disposed of in the 1950–53 period, only the 'Old Trafford' going on to service elsewhere. Quite why the 'Rixton' was retained for so long is not clear, but she was eventually sold for conversion to a barge at Liverpool, renamed the 'White Star,' and broken up at Widnes in 1975.

The paddle tugs were withdrawn with the arrival of new and more powerful twin-screw vessels built by Henry Robb Ltd., and fitted with Crossley diesel engines. An example is the M.S.C. 'Panther,' delivered in 1950, seen here approaching Eastham Locks. The use of tugs, which were hired from the Company, depended largely upon the length and beam of the vessel under tow. Communication between ship's crew, or pilot, and the tugs was initially by sound signals (ship's siren or whistle) until radio telephones came into use. Radio control centres were also used to record and regulate the movement of shipping on the canal.

Four tugs of a new hydroconic hull design, built at Appledore by P.K.Harris Ltd., were delivered in 1956–57. They boasted a spacious wheelhouse with a clear view aft, and proved extremely manoeuvrable. The traditional funnel had been replaced by a tripod mast, the outside legs of which doubled as exhausts for the twin engines. M.S.C. 'Sceptre' and 'Sabre' prepare to pull the Harrison liner 'Plainsman' into the canal from Eastham Locks. It normally took a large ship about 20 minutes to clear the lock after Customs and Tolls. Pilotage in the Mersey is compulsory, although not obligatory in the canal. Pilots are self-employed and, if required, could be booked to join the ship at Eastham as the Mersey pilots left. Helmsmen could be obtained in the same manner.

A 1958 aerial view of Barton with the aqueduct and road bridge open to permit the passage of a freighter inward bound for Manchester. By this date, the increase in the number of road vehicles caused traffic queues whenever the bridge was swung. The line of the Bridgewater Canal may be noted. Brindley's 1761 aqueduct crossed at a point between the two swing bridges. Barton Power Station (top left), now demolished, received much of its coal supply via Bridgewater Canal barges.

At Runcorn, the lack of a road bridge to Widnes had been solved by the provision of a Transporter Bridge in 1905. Towers on each bank supported a high-level girder span, on which ran a trolley operated by electric motors. Suspended on cables below the trolley was a travelling platform, capable of carrying pedestrians, animals, carts, and motor vehicles. The scheduled service operated every 20 minutes, but by the 1950s the transporter was inadequate for the number of users, and it was dismantled after a new road bridge opened in 1961. The transporter is seen here in the 1950s, with the tug 'Quarry' passing by on the Ship Canal. The travelling platform may be noted arriving at the Runcorn side, where it had a clearance of only a few feet over the wall of the canal. Its progress was controlled by an operator on the platform, who had to have due regard for traffic on the canal.

Irlam Ferry M.S.C. 'Traverse' is passed by the Furness Withy liner 'Pacific Reliance.' The 'Pacific Reliance' was the second ship to carry this name. It was built in 1951 and traded along the canal for twenty years until sold to Belgian shipbreakers in 1971.

No.9 Dock in the peak years, seen from the No.2 Grain Elevator end, is crowded with ships of all nations. Three floating pneumatic elevators suck grain from the holds of ships from North America, and discharge into lighters alongside, probably for forward passage via Hulme Locks into the Bridgewater Canal for the Kelloggs factory in Trafford Park.

# THE 1960s

Any blockage of the canal was potentially very serious, in that it restricted access to Manchester. On the 22nd March 1961 the sand hopper 'Mary P. Cooper' was in collision, and sank near Stockton Heath. Small and medium-sized vessels managed to squeeze past the obstruction, but larger ships were trapped in the upper reaches of the canal for several days. This was the scene on the 8th April when the salvage boat 'Dispenser' had arrived from Southampton and divers were attaching cables to the wreck. Fortunately, incidents of this sort were few, but another stoppage was caused in March 1969, when the 'Manchester Courage,' outward bound for Montreal, ran into and burst open the lower lock gates at Irlam. Apart from the damage to the lock, the accident also caused the level of water to fall in the stretch of the canal between Irlam and Barton. It was some five weeks before normal traffic could be resumed, during which time large ships were detained in the terminal docks.

In the early 1960s the old bucket-dredger 'Irwell' was replaced by a new vessel of the same name. The new 'Irwell' operated mainly in the section between Warrington and Manchester, removing some 900,000 cubic yards of silt annually. The sludge was transported in barges to a pumping station at Thelwall, where it was diluted with water and pumped to deposit grounds. The new vessel is seen at Old Quay, Runcorn, with launch 'Diana' alongside. Though having one of the dirtiest jobs, the 'Irwell' was one of the cleanest and best-maintained vessels on the canal.

The age of steam on the railways was coming to an end in the 1960s. The last steam locomotives purchased by the Ship Canal Company were three saddle-tanks, numbered 89–90, manufactured in 1954 by Hudswell Clarke of Leeds. They remained in service for only ten years. Number 90 here crosses the railway swing bridge about 1962 with a train of tobacco en route for the bonded warehouses in Trafford Park.

An odd item of rolling stock on the Ship Canal railway was the cashiers' coach. Workers along the canal between Salford and Old Quay, received their wages from a launch, the 'Dispatch,' up to 1945, but thereafter by locomotive to Latchford and hire car to Runcorn. A second-hand coach was obtained, the first of three, and suitably fitted out for the job. The locomotive is number 84, a Hunslet engine delivered in 1931.

Steam locomotives began to be replaced by diesel from 1959 onwards, most withdrawals taking place between 1963 and 1967. This was the sad scene at Mode Wheel in April 1966, when lines of steam engines were being cut up for scrap. The remains of number 53 ('Sweden') stand in front of number 22 ('Rotterdam').

The end of steam on the dock railways came in 1967. Locomotive number 32 (formerly 'Gothenburg' of 1903, and now preserved by the East Lancashire Light Railway Company, Bury), shunts a train of cargo for Montreal on No.9 Dock, alongside the 'Manchester Mariner.' The date is 6th July 1966.

A total of 40 diesel locomotives were purchased between 1959 and 1966. D13, a Hudswell Clarke product of 1962, and DH17, a Rolls Royce Sentinel of 1964, stand outside the shed at Mode Wheel in 1966. At this date, the shed behind was still full of lifeless steam engines. By 1980, most of the diesel locomotives had been sold or scrapped, only nine remaining on the dock estate and five on the Ellesmere Port-Stanlow lines.

Coastwise traffic continued to use Pomona Docks, and at No.3 Dock a heavy lift berth was established. Roll-on, roll-off facilities were available for ships designed for the transport of very heavy loads of up to 300 tons per unit. The 'Aberthaw Fisher,' a 'Ro-Ro' vessel of James Fisher & Sons, specially adapted for such cargoes, is seen in Pomona in 1966.

The docks in 1966 showed optimistic signs of expansion. A new storage shed was under construction on No.6 Dock South (bottom left), many ships were using the port, and railway connections were busy. Manchester Liners had invested in another new ship, the third 'Manchester Port,' specially strengthened for ice-breaking in order to operate a round-the-year service to Montreal. The Liners owned or had on charter no fewer than 20 vessels. Sadly, the ambitious programme of development was disrupted. In May-July 1966 the National Union of Seamen called a strike which lasted for 47 days, crews leaving their vessels as they returned to Britain. Of the seven large ships moored in Nos.6 and 7 Docks, four are vessels belonging to Manchester Liners, laid up with the others awaiting the end of the strike.

Cayzer Irvine 'Clan Line' steamers had been coming to Manchester since 1895, when Sir Charles Cayzer had been energetic in establishing a regular service to and from Indian Ocean ports. 'Clan Graham' (built 1962) was the first ship to use the new transit shed in No.6 Dock on the 6th July 1967. The new shed had been designed so that mechanical handling equipment could operate at peak efficiency.

An unusual sort of export was seen on No.9 Dock in September 1967, when the 60-ton floating crane loaded an old tramcar on to the 'Manchester Renown' for delivery to the United States. Blackpool tramcar number 147, built in 1924, was on its way to a transport museum in Colombia Park, Cleveland, Ohio. There had been a precedent just over a year earlier, when the 'Manchester Progress' had carried six vintage narrow-gauge locomotives from the Penrhyn Quarries for a railway museum in Virginia.

At the western end of the canal, the new Vauxhall Motors plant at Ellesmere Port was conveniently close to the dock. In April 1968 the vessel 'La Primavera' was loading 850 cars for export to Canada. At this time, the vehicles were placed individually in a cradle, and then lifted by crane over the side of the ship. Later, a ramp was provided and specially-designed ships, with several car decks, simplified the loading process. The docks at Ellesmere Port, the terminus of the Shropshire Union Canal, were leased to the Ship Canal Company by the British Waterways Board.

Bowater's Pulp & Paper Mills established their own wharf between Ellesmere Port and Eastham. The 'Bright Moon' unloads timber in June 1969. Part of Mount Manisty is seen to the right of the photograph.

In 1968 the Prince Line, whose ships had been using the canal since its opening in 1894, withdrew its loss-making Manchester services, and in November 1970 Furness Withy likewise closed its Manchester–North Pacific routes. The Prince Line's Mediterranean services were taken over by Manchester Liners with three ships on long-term charter. Manchester Liners also attempted to stem the rising costs and falling productivity of shore workers, whose disruptive strikes had exacerbated the problem, by pioneering the change to container traffic for the Canadian services. Three ships were commissioned from Smith's Dock Company, Middlesbrough, the first cellular container vessels to be built by a British shipyard. Subsequently, an additional vessel was ordered, together with 10,000 containers. Efficiency was increased by exclusive control of terminals in Manchester

and Montreal, ensuring the quick turn-round of vessels. Conventional ships were sold off or converted as the new container vessels arrived. First to be delivered in late-1968 was the 'Manchester Challenge,' whose bow is seen here by the new gantry crane and container storage area, sited on the former timber ground on the north side of No.9 Dock.

The 'Manchester Courage' was the second vessel built to the new design, which took into account the limitations of the Ship Canal, aiming for maximum capacity, a brief passage, and the shortest possible time in port. The ships had 14 hatches and five separate holds, with space for 500 containers. Initially, because of the North Atlantic weather, it had been decided to carry all containers below deck.

To maintain a winter service to Montreal, an 'ice knife' was fitted aft over the rudder to offer protection if the ships had to back into the ice. The container traffic, begun in November 1968, soon developed into a regular, twice-weekly service, taking 6½ days to cross to the 'gateway' port of Montreal, where smaller container vessels served as 'feeders' to and from the Great Lakes ports. The introduction of containers stabilised costs, and reduced pilferage and damage. Time in port was cut from ten days or more, to two, or even less. To help preserve jobs on the docks, the containers were, when necessary, 'stuffed' (i.e. given a full load, rather be carried partly empty) or 'unstuffed' on land just behind the terminal. A second gantry crane was provided in 1971 as trade increased. The Mediterranean services were also converted to container traffic, the smaller number of vessels carrying more than twice as much cargo as the conventional ships of the 1950s and '60s.

# DECLINE AND REVITALISATION OF THE DOCKLANDS

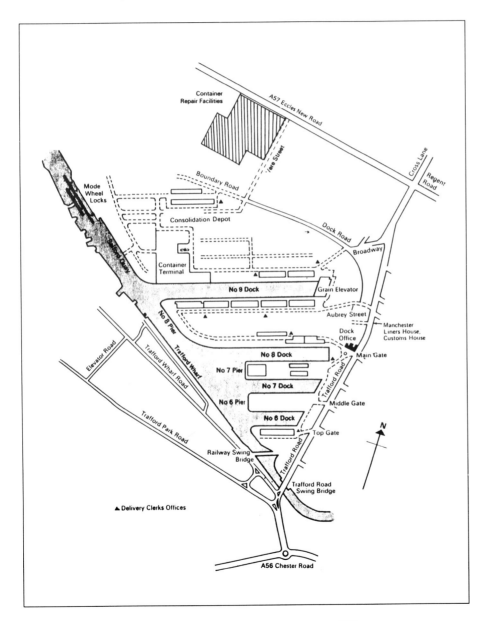

Plan of Manchester Docks in the 1970s.

The small ports at the western end of the canal enjoyed a boom period when the motorway network was extended into North Cheshire. The onward carriage of imports by road to inland destinations was thus facilitated, but some canal traffic to Manchester was reduced because of its distance from the sea and the time taken in the passage of the canal. A container terminal was established at Ellesmere Port, where a motorway link ran directly into the dock estate. The old docks at Runcorn, seen here crowded with small ships in the early 1970s, were well able to deal with general cargo, but began to specialise in the handling of bulk commodities or palletised loads. Runcorn Docks, which could accommodate vessels up to 350 feet in length, were improved with a widened entrance. The main imports became steel, crude minerals, fertilizers, and chemicals, whilst exports were salt, chemicals, and machinery. The graceful arch of the 1961 road bridge may be noted beyond the railway viaduct. Bridgewater House, occupied by the Duke during the construction of the Bridgewater Canal, lies between the docks and the bridge.

Unusual, but regular out-of-season visitors to the canal were boats of the Isle Of Man Steam Packet Company, on their way to the Dry Docks at Manchester for winter maintenance work. The 'Ben-My-Chree,' a turbine car ferry (built 1966), enters the canal at Eastham, drawn along by the tug M.S.C. 'Victory' in the late 1970s.

Other occasional visitors sailing the length of the canal were Mersey ferry boats. They were often hired on summer weekends by the Co-Operative Travel Agency for trips from Liverpool Landing Stage to Pomona Docks, passengers returning by rail. On the following day, another party would make the trip in the opposite direction as the ferry returned to Liverpool. The 'Egremont' is seen here on a trip about 1975. Such excursions continue, but now terminate at Mode Wheel.

In 1894 the Port of Manchester had handled 925,000 tons of traffic. In the period 1954–74 the annual total regularly exceeded 16,000,000 tons, and over 5000 ships entered the waterway each year. Vessels of up to 12,500 tons deadweight could navigate to Manchester, but in the 1970s the number of large ships passing all the way along the canal began to decline. The troubles of the 1960s continued in 1971 with a series of unofficial strikes by dock workers, and in 1972 there was a national dock strike lasting four weeks. Problems continued intermittently throughout the decade, and customers took their cargoes away. Manchester Liners traded at a loss in 1971 and 1972. The resulting lack of confidence on the part of shippers was a factor in the decline of Manchester as a port. On the Bridgewater Canal, the last barge load of maize imported via Manchester Docks for Kelloggs in Trafford Park on the 29th March 1974, marked the end of commercial use of the smaller waterway. A fierce rate-cutting war between shippers on the North Atlantic run in the late 1970s, plus a depressed market, did not help matters. Clan Line vessels continued to put in an occasional appearance. In July 1977 'Clan Macgregor' towed by the tug M.S.C. 'Viceroy' (new in 1975) passes the 'Daniel Adamson,' whose catering staff are preparing to receive an official party.

The 'Daniel Adamson' is a unique survivor. Built for the Shropshire Union Canal Company in 1903 as the 'Ralph Brocklebank,' she was designed to tow barges across the Mersey estuary from Ellesmere Port to Liverpool. In 1922 she passed into the ownership of the Ship Canal Company, and, having some passenger accommodation, became the canal tender. In 1936 she was refurbished and given the name of the first chairman of the Company, who had hitherto lacked any memorial. At one time in regular use for canal inspections, as well as being available for general towing duties as required, the 'Daniel Adamson' retained steam-driven machinery long after it had been superseded elsewhere. Now to be found at the Boat Museum, Ellesmere Port, the tug is seen near Barton in 1981, carrying a visiting party.

Traffic on the upper reaches of the Ship Canal had dwindled to such an extent that the company considered complete closure of the section above Runcorn. Manchester Liners, since 1970 a subsidiary of Furness Withy, faced losses and was troubled by mergers and take-over bids. The Canadian service ceased to operate from Manchester in 1979. Furness Withy itself was sold to the Hong Kong-based C. Y. Tung Group in 1980. Soon, there were only three ships bearing the 'Manchester' name, the 'Manchester Challenge,' on the North Atlantic run, the 'Manchester Crown' and the 'Manchester Trader' on the Mediterranean service, all working out of Ellesmere Port, 33 miles nearer the sea. Some 3000 dockers' jobs had vanished. The last Manchester Liners vessels were sold by 1985, and the Company lost its shipping interests. In 1988 the services formerly operated by Manchester Liners were integrated into the Orient Overseas Container Line, successor to the Tung Group. The Canal Company had suffered from falling revenue as trade moved elsewhere, and faced greater losses in the 1980s. Amongst the last regular users of the upper section of the waterway were the North West Water Authority sludge boats 'Percy Dawson' and 'Gilbert J. Fowler,' and even they continued only until the completion of a pipeline from the Davyhulme treatment works. The tidal estuary of the Mersey is seen beyond the slender embankment in this view near Stanlow Point.

Because of the small number of ships using the canal, the overhead costs of maintenance seemed to grow out of proportion. Dredging still had to be carried out. The grab dredger 'Donald Redford' (named after the Company Chairman 1972–85) was at work near Stanlow in October 1984.

In the 1970s Corn Products (now Cerestar U.K.) of Trafford Park, chartered a large bulk carrier to import grain. By the 1980s the grain was transhipped at the Seaforth Grain Terminal into smaller vessels. In 1984, by courtesy of the Ship Canal Company's Public

Relations Officer, the writer was privileged to join the crew of the 'Seacombe Trader' for a trip on what was thought would be one of the last regular commercial passages along the upper reaches of the canal. It was anticipated that the service would cease, and that the grain would be delivered by road. In fact, at the time of writing, the grain is still imported via the canal, but under European Common Market regulations, now comes from France. The view is along the deck of the 'Seacombe Trader' as it rises in Barton Locks. The bridge of the M63 Motorway, built 82 feet above normal water level in 1960 to clear the ocean-going ships which then passed beneath it, stands between the locks and the Barton swing bridge.

By the early 1980s, although the future for the lower reaches of the canal seemed assured, with an expectation of some 3000 ships per year using the western-end ports, shippers who had used Manchester Docks had either closed down or moved away because the canal could not accommodate the larger vessels then coming into use. The Ship Canal Company knew that traffic would not return, and that continued operation of the upper reaches would result in an even greater loss than had been experienced thus far. In the December 1984 issue of the 'Port Of Manchester Review,' the Company Chairman, Donald Redford, wrote: "Since the original purpose of Manchester Docks has gone, what of the future? It is good sense and good business to explore and attract new uses and jobs. Nearly all the dock estate lies in Salford and much of it is in the Enterprise Zone. Some has been sold to the Salford City Council. To prepare the way for redevelopment, the massive grain elevator and other buildings have been demolished, rail tracks taken up and new drainage and estate roads laid out."

The result has been the Salford Quays development, a mixture of high-quality residential, business, hotel and leisure interests, which has transformed the derelict quaysides. The old docks have been divided into water parks, alongside which attractive houses and striking new office blocks have arisen. New, smaller canals link the former docks, giving a Dutch air to the estate. Water quality has been improved, and the former No.7 Dock is now stocked by Salford City Council with fish, forming a mecca for weekend anglers. There is a marina for pleasure craft, and the on-going programme includes plans for a performing arts centre between the former Nos.8 and 9 Docks. 'Harbour City' clusters around the old No.9 Dock.

The new 'Mariners Canal' links the former No.8 Dock (now 'Ontario Basin') with the old No.9 Dock ('Erie Basin'). Residential property lining the new canal is known as 'Grain Wharf.' The large building at the head, standing on the far side of the former No.9 Dock, is the 'Victoria' office block of 'Harbour City.' The new names chosen for the water basins reflect the former trade connection with the Great Lakes of North America.

Ships of a different sort are still to be seen in the former No.8 Dock. A visiting attraction in 1993 was the replica of Drake's ship 'The Golden Hinde,' whilst radio-controlled model yachts offer entertainment for enthusiasts on Sunday mornings. The tall office block is the former Manchester Liners House of 1969 (since renamed Furness House), which was designed to resemble the bridge of a ship.

Across the old No.9 Dock, separating 'Huron Basin' from 'Erie Basin,' is the former railway swing bridge, transported from its former location and fixed to provide pedestrian access from the residential property on the left to the commercial office developments of 'Harbour City' on the other side.

The minesweeper H.M.S. 'Bronington,' formerly commanded by H.R.H. Prince Charles, is moored at Trafford Wharf, offering another attraction for visitors.

The construction of the Manchester Ship Canal was the greatest engineering project of Victorian times. It was successful in making Manchester one of the major ports of the world and in bringing prosperity to the region. The Canal Company's income came from two main sources, namely ships' dues and cargo handling charges. Ships' dues were payable by the owner of any vessel entering or leaving the port, while cargo dues (canal tolls) were payable by the cargo owner. Rates were assessed according to tonnage and the length of canal used (Eastham-Runcorn, Eastham-Latchford, or Eastham-Manchester), though latterly divided into two sections (Eastham-Runcorn and Runcorn-Manchester). The total tonnage of goods handled reached a maximum in the late 1950s, but by the 1980s, after almost 90 years of operation, Manchester Docks fell victim to competition in a declining market for ship and cargo handling services. The Canal Company has now moved its Post Division headquarters to Runcorn, where traffic on the lower reaches

is handled profitably and efficiently, and has diversified interests in, for example, property development at Salford Quays and a proposed new shopping centre at Barton. At the time of writing, a new road bridge is being built to cross the canal between Trafford Park and Eccles. It is designed to have a lifting centre section, so that ships can continue to navigate to Salford Quays.

Though the upper reaches of the canal are no longer busy, there are still some steady traffics, notably grain, oil and chemical products and scrap, and the dry docks operated by Lengthline Limited just within Salford Quays, continue to provide a graving and repair service. On the 28th February 1993, the coastal tanker 'Gordon Thomas' is escorted from Mode Wheel locks by tugs 'Viceroy' and 'Volant' on its way for maintenance work in the dry docks. Since 1989 the four remaining tugs (the two pictured, plus 'Victory' and 'Viking') have been operated by Carmet Tugs Limited.

# BIBLIOGRAPHY

Bracegirdle, Cyril *The Dark River* Sherratt, Altrincham 1973.

Bruce, Warren J. *With The Manchester Ship Canal Company, 1894–1945* Neil Richardson, Salford 1990.

Corbett, J. *The River Irwell* Manchester 1907.

Corbridge, J. *A Pictorial History Of The Mersey & Irwell Navigation* Morten, Manchester 1979.

Farnie, D. A. *The Manchester Ship Canal and the rise of the Port of Manchester 1894-1975* Manchester 1980.

Frangopulo, N. *Tradition In Action* E.P.Publishing, Wakefield 1977.

Hallam, W. B. *Tugs Of The Manchester Ship Canal* M.S.C.Co. 1978.

Hayman, Alfred *Mersey & Irwell Navigation To Manchester Ship Canal* Federation of Bridgewater Cruising Clubs 1981.

Leech, Sir Bosdin *The History Of The Manchester Ship Canal* Sherratt, Altrincham 1907.

Lees, Barrie *The People's Canal* Eccles Journal, June–October 1977.

Makepiece, Chris *The Manchester Ship Canal — A Short History* Hendon Publishing Company, Nelson 1983.

Malet, Hugh *Bridgewater — The Canal Duke 1736–1803* Manchester University Press 1977.

McMurray, H. Campbell *Old Order, New Thing* National Maritime Museum, Greenwich/HMSO 1972.

Mullineux, F. *The Duke Of Bridgewater's Canal* Eccles 1959

Owen, David *The Manchester Ship Canal* Manchester University Press 1983.

Stoker, R. B. *The Saga Of Manchester Liners* Kinglish, Isle Of Man 1985.

Thorpe, D. *The Railways Of The Manchester Ship Canal* Oxford 1984.

Tracy, W. B. et al *Port Of Manchester, 1708–1901* Manchester 1901.

Periodicals include the *Port Of Manchester Review* (the annual house magazine of the Company) and the *Port Of Manchester Sailing List and Guide*.

# CHRONOLOGY OF PRINCIPAL EVENTS 1710–1905

1710 ..... First mention of a Ship Canal from Manchester to the sea.

1712 ..... Steers' scheme for deepening the rivers Mersey and Irwell.

1721 ..... Act obtained for the Mersey & Irwell Navigation scheme.

1734 ..... Ships of up to 50 tons able to sail to Manchester via the Mersey and Irwell Navigation.

1759 ..... Work began at Worsley on the Duke of Bridgewater's Canal.

1764 ..... Bridgewater Canal open to Castlefield, Manchester.

1766 ..... Passenger-carrying services began on Bridgewater Canal.

1776 ..... Bridgewater Canal extended to Runcorn.

1796 ..... Duke of Bridgewater's experimental steamboat planned.

1804 ..... Runcorn & Latchford Canal opened, improving access to Mersey for vessels using the Mersey & Irwell river navigation.

1807 ..... Passenger-carrying services began on Mersey & Irwell system.

1816 ..... Steamboats introduced (at first for passengers only) on the Mersey estuary between Runcorn and Liverpool. Some steam tugs used from 1824 to tow barges across the estuary.

1825 ..... Application to cut a canal via Lymm to the Dee estuary refused.

1830 ..... Opening of the Liverpool & Manchester Railway.

1838 ..... Rennie's report on a Ship Canal from Liverpool to Warrington, which could be extended to Manchester.

1839 ..... Manchester & Salford Junction Canal opened.

1840 ..... Palmer and Bateman presented two schemes for a Ship Canal.

1844 ..... Bridgewater Trustees bought the Mersey & Irwell Navigation system.

1872 ..... Bridgewater Canal and the Mersey & Irwell River Navigation bought by the Bridgewater Navigation Company, which was dominated by railway shareholders. E.Leader Williams appointed General Manager and Engineer. Steam tugs introduced on Bridgewater Canal; river navigation neglected.

1876 ..... George Hicks' letter to the *'Manchester Guardian'* suggesting that rivers Mersey and Irwell should be converted into a Ship Canal.

1877 ..... Manchester Chamber of Commerce considered Fulton's scheme for an improved waterway from the sea.

1879 ..... Manchester businessmen voted in favour of a Ship Canal.

1881 ..... Salford Town Council debated a motion about improving the Irwell.

1882 ..... Pamphlets published urging a tidal navigation to Manchester.

27th June 1882 ............Meeting convened by Daniel Adamson; Provisional Ship Canal Committee, representing merchants, manufacturers, and municipal authorities formed to consider tidal navigation.

17th August 1882 ........Inspection of the route of the proposed waterway.

26th September 1882 ...Rejection of tidal proposal and adoption of Leader Williams' scheme for large canal with locks.

6th July 1883 ..............First Bill passed by Commons; later rejected by Lords.

24th May 1884 ...........Second Bill passed by Lords; later rejected by Commons.

6th August 1885 .........Third Bill received Royal assent.

3rd August 1887 .........Bridgewater Navigation Company purchased.

11th November 1887 ...Work on construction of Ship Canal commenced, with Leader Williams as Engineer-in-Chief and Thomas A.Walker as contractor.

25th November 1889 ...Contractor T.A.Walker died; works and plant subsequently taken over by the Company.

13th January 1890 .......Daniel Adamson died, aged 71.

19th June 1891 ...........Water first admitted into a section of the Canal from the estuary near Ellesmere Port.

2nd July 1891 ..............Water admitted into Eastham Locks.

16th July 1891 ............Traffic to Ellesmere Port via the Ship Canal commenced.

28th September 1891 ...Ship Canal open to Weston Marsh Lock for River Weaver traffic.
[Work on Runcorn section then commenced.]

22nd July 1892 ...........Saltport established.

13th December 1892 ...Trafford Road Bridge, the heaviest swing bridge in the country, sucessfully turned for the first time.

9th January 1893 .........Cheshire Lines viaduct at Irlam opened for goods traffic.

27th February 1893 ......Railway viaducts at Acton Grange, Latchford and Cadishead opened for goods traffic.

27th March 1893 ........Cheshire Lines railway viaduct at Irlam opened for passenger traffic.

29th May 1893 ...........Cheshire Lines viaduct at Cadishead opened for passenger traffic.

9th June 1893 .............Water admitted into the Runcorn section.

8th July 1893 ..............Water admitted into the Canal between Runcorn Docks and Old Quay.

9th July 1893 ..............Viaducts at Acton Grange and Latchford opened for passenger traffic, thus releasing the last piece of land required to be cut through.

17th November 1893 ...Water admitted into the Canal between Runcorn and Latchford.

25th November 1893 ...Canal filled from end to end 10.30pm

7th December 1893 .....First journey of Directors by water over whole length of Canal.

lst January 1894 ..........Canal opened for traffic to Manchester.

21st May 1894 .............Formal opening of Canal by Queen Victoria.

15th August 1904 ........Bill for increasing depth of Canal from 26 to 28 feet.

13th July 1905 .............Dock No.9 opened on site of old Manchester Racecourse.

# INDEX

# Available From All Good Book Shops
## by Ted Gray

*Ted Gray*

# Available From All Good Book Shops

£3.75

Ted Gray

£4.95